"It will probably make you uncomfortable to see branding juxtaposed with religion, but the fact is that religions have been doing marketing since the very beginning of time. Just ask Zeus or Thor . . . ideas that spread, win."

SETH GODIN
AUTHOR, *LINCHPIN*

"Here are helpful words from a fellow pastor whose church uniquely reaches its community and touches people's lives with the love of God. Kumar Dixit encourages church leaders to discover how their church's identity in the community profoundly affects its presentation of the gospel—and what they can do about it."

NATHAN SPECK-EWER
LEAD PASTOR, ST. TIMOTHY'S EPISCOPAL CHURCH
MOUNTAIN VIEW, CALIFORNIA

"Churches are struggling today to find their way in a very changed context. Those church leaders who are guiding their congregations and denominations successfully are thinking about the questions Kumar Dixit is raising in this book. Readers will find ways to respond to what he writes in ways as varied as are their traditions, but respond they must."

LOVETT H. WEEMS JR.
DIRECTOR, LEWIS CENTER FOR CHURCH LEADERSHIP
WESLEY THEOLOGICAL SEMINARY

"*Branded Faith* reminds the reader that though the church once led the way in art, politics, and commerce, it has been struggling to keep up ever since. Kumar Dixit implores the faith to learn from industry and adapt in order to stay relevant—all the while facing the challenge to not lose its soul in the process."

RAJEEV SIGAMONEY
HOLLYWOOD FILMMAKER
WRITER/PRODUCER OF *JESUS PEOPLE* FILM

"As someone who has seen audiences all over the country respond in remarkable ways to the story of Scripture presented dramatically, I certainly resonate with Pastor Kumar Dixit's message about rebranding through storytelling. It's an important principle for us absorb."

STEVEN MOSLEY
TELEVISION PRODUCER, SPEAKER

"Kumar Dixit has little interest in a church that spends its resources on talking to 'the saints' and keeping them comfortable. In this lively, practical book, he passionately envisions a church out on the streets, bravely and creatively shaping the good news in honest and meaningful ways that help connect people to God. Anyone interested in a church that's more than a club should read this book."

GARY KRAUSE
DIRECTOR OF ADVENTIST MISSION
AUTHOR, GOD'S GREAT MISSIONARIES

"At the leading edge of thinking about how to help the Church speak in today's marketplace is Kumar Dixit. Kumar is a faithful Christian leader offering new insight and ideas about how to help church leaders and people in the pew make the gospel accessible to the "McWorld" we live in. His spiritual leadership and guidance is creative and fresh and will inspire Christians to share faith!"

REVEREND ERIKA O. GARA
LEAD PASTOR, HOPE UMC
TORRANCE, CALIFORNIA

"As a radio chaplain who deals with hundreds of thousands of people weekly, I find Dr. Rajkumar Dixit writings to be real, relevant, and relational. I would recommend this book to anyone who deals with people and wants to inspire them."

CHAPLAIN TERRY LYNDON JOHNSSON
WGTS 91.9 FM
AUTHOR, AIM HIGH

"This book will not rest idly on the bookshelf. It will engage and re-engage church leaders of every stripe. Kumar's keen interpretation of the times, practical guidance, and sense of humor promise to challenge, aid, and encourage us for years to come. Anyone who cares about the present and future of the church will find a wise companion in Kumar Dixit."

REVEREND ANDREW NAGY-BENSON
UNITED CHRIST OF CHRIST CONGREGATION
LECTURER, YALE UNIVERSITY

"How a church "brands" and "markets" itself in the world has so much to do with its sense of identity and mission. Kumar Dixit's head-turning insights and thought-provoking proposals on the rebranding of Christian communities will challenge the pervasive church-as-usual mentality and move his readers toward a fresh examination of how their churches are living out their identities and mission in the world."

JULIUS NAM, PHD
PROFESSOR, LOMA LINDA UNIVERSITY

"Kumar Dixit is passionate about the church's relevance, reputation, and reach. *Branded Faith* is a book that will pique the interest of church leaders who desire to reach their communities in today's generation."

DR. DAVID ANDERSON
BRIDGEWAY COMMUNITY CHURCH
AUTHOR, *GRACISM: THE ART OF INCLUSION*

"Articulate and accessible, Dixit's *Branded Faith* offers an insightful investigation of the church's loss of societal identity. The writing is on the wall for the declining church, however Dixit pens a viable intervention that has the potential to invigorate the distinctiveness of the faith community. In the white noise of today's cultural milieu, *Branded Faith* makes a significant mark."

A. ALLEN MARTIN, PHD
AUTHOR, *GOD ENCOUNTERS*

"Kumar Dixit writes as a seasoned practitioner in ministry. His perspective is shaped by on-the-ground experience and is one that the church today truly needs to hear."

DENISE VAN ECK
AUTHOR

Branded Faith

Branded Faith

Contextualizing the Gospel in a Post-Christian Era

RAJKUMAR DIXIT

WIPF & STOCK · Eugene, Oregon

BRANDED FAITH
Contextualizing the Gospel in a Post-Christian Era

Wipf & Stock
An Imprint of Wipf and Stock Publishers
199 W. 8th Ave., Suite 3
Eugene, OR 97401
www.wipfandstock.com

ISBN 13: 978-1-60899-559-2

Manufactured in the U.S.A.

Dedicated to Gloria Dixit,
my mother.
Thank you for never giving up on your prayers
for a troubled teenage son.
God listened. God extended his grace.
With love, your son.

Contents

Foreword

I KNOW RAJKUMAR (KUMAR) Dixit as a neighbor. We live and serve in the same cluster of neighborhoods that stretch between Washington DC, and Baltimore, Maryland. Although we come from different Christian traditions, our differences add interest to our relationship, not division. After all, it would be kind of boring to only have friends who are exactly like you, don't you think?

Because we live in the same area, we see similar problems. We see the huge gap between the subcultures of most of our Christian communities and the general culture shared by most of the people of our region, most of whom won't be in any church this weekend. We see how the kinds of arguments and debates that animate religious communities have virtually no overlap with the issues that engage the attention and energy of our nonreligious neighbors. The spiritual needs and honest questions of our secular neighbors get through to us, and we want to see our churches do a better job of meeting those needs and answering those questions.

In the chapters you're about to read, Kumar will introduce you to a number of true stories from the worlds of business and marketing; he'll invite you to gain insights from those worlds that can be applied to the worlds of Christian faith and mission. In so doing, he's not just making a late addition to the pile of church-growth books that were especially popular back in the 1990s. Nor is he dumbing down the gospel into a product, degrading disciples into consumers of religious goods and services, or demoting the art of Christian communication into a peppy infomercial. He's doing something more thoughtful than that.

For example, in the coming chapters, he'll lead you effortlessly from a study of the rise and stumble of the Starbucks brand in America to a thoughtful overview of Paul's communication strategy in the ancient Mediterranean world. You won't be offered shallow gimmicks and tricks for fast and easy growth; instead you'll be challenged to think in fresh and needed ways about real and lasting mission in your community . . . mission that must begin with communication, which must in turn begin with better understanding both of the people around you and of the communication process itself.

If it was fashionable in the 1990s to turn pastors into CEO's, seekers into consumers of religious goods and services, and church services into niche-marketing infomercials with peppy music, it was equally fashionable in the 2000s to react against learning anything at all from the worlds of business and marketing. Perhaps this book represents a hopeful trend in the 2010s: to realize that although the church shouldn't be reduced to a business, it certainly shouldn't be run like a bad business. From both the successes and failures of businesses, then, we can gain some needed insight to help us in our work of communication.

Kumar has read widely and deeply in both business and theology, as you'll see. Equally important, he loves the local church and he's in it up to his elbows—pastoring, leading, studying, testing out his ideas. On top of that, he writes with clarity and passion to help Christians, church leaders, and denominational leaders move wisely from reflection into action. For these reasons and more, I'm glad that *Branded Faith* will be available to Christian leaders who want to share the good news of Jesus with people outside the doors of our churches . . . even if it might mean (as you'll soon discover) adding some ashtrays on the front step.

Brian McLaren
Laurel, Maryland
www.brianmclaren.net

Acknowledgments

SOME PEOPLE ARE BORN writers. They write from their hearts and everything that appears on the written page seems eloquent and organic. I am not a natural writer. In fact, I am self-conscious of everything I put on paper; I would much rather preach, speak, or present than write. Writing is a solitary act—done in the privacy of your mind; not shared until it is presentable. This can cause difficulty for an extreme extrovert like me, However, the passion I have for this particular topic seemed to carry me through the difficult days of writing. I am grateful to the following people who championed my endeavors:

Rajinie—for supporting me through the process of writing. You listened to my ideas while I was sorting them out. I know much of this church leadership jargon was not too interesting to you, but thanks for allowing me the space and time.

Jay and Saramma Sigamoney—for supporting my ministry. I can't think of a better set of in-laws. Thank you for sacrificing your personal time and work to watch the kids so Rej and I could get a break. More than anything, thanks for Wednesday night Chapati.

Reema—my darling sister who is always willing to pick up the phone numerous times a day to listen to the crazy ramblings of her little bro—thanks!

Katina Chappell—for editing and re-editing. Thank you for getting rid of the red pen and using pencil. My self-esteem was saved as a result. Also, thank you for allowing Marty to join us for the Cheesecake Factory outings. You are such a generous friend.

Dr. J. David Newman—I have worked for more than thirteen senior pastors, and you come out on top. Your encouragement through this writing process has been welcome. Thank you for reading and editing my chapters and giving me your critical feedback.

My dear friend, Bub. Thank you for encouraging me throughout this project. Your desire for the church to demonstrate excellence has fueled me. Also, thanks for the inspiration for the front cover. I am grateful.

The pastoral staff at New Hope Church—Richard Anderson, Jr.; David Gemmell; Ann Roda; Lynne Ekelof; Prithy David; Elizabeth Moore; Eunice de Jesus; and Collier Rowe—you have been a blast to work with. Thank you for giving me the flexibility to write and for picking up my slack when I fell behind in my work.

Anne Woodworth—for reading my first drafts and making corrections without laughing or making cruel comments. You have been such a joy to work with. Thanks for believing in me from the very start of this venture.

A. Grace Brown—for copyediting this book and for going the extra mile. Thank you for your detailed eye and careful critique.

To the members of New Hope Church, thank you for letting me use you as guinea pigs. Your faithfulness and commitment to reaching your friends and family for Christ has been inspiring. Thank you for willing to try almost anything for God's kingdom.

PART ONE

1

Adapting to the Audience

The reason some folks don't believe in missions is that the brand of religion they have isn't worth propagating.

—UNKNOWN

REV. TODD THOMASON HAD a major crisis on his hands. Every week he looked out at his congregation to see only a handful of parishioners in attendance. The robust congregation at Baptist Temple Church in Alexandria, Virginia, which once boasted a membership of nine hundred, was long gone. Thomason confronted this reality every Sunday as he faced the thirty members who still regularly attended. In response to this drastic decline, the church was desperately considering its options.

One of the options being explored was a name change, in hopes that this would bring the church one step closer to reaching the community. As reported in an article in the *Washington Post*, the congregation felt that the name "Baptist" created preconceived notions about the church and carried a negative connotation because of personal scandals involving high profile religious leaders such as Jerry Falwell and Tammy Faye Bakker. Moreover, "There is a kind of national skepticism about evangelical Christianity because of the Religious Right and the connection to the Bush administration. You say, 'Baptist' and people almost automatically think conservative," says David Roozen, director of the Hartford Institute for Religion. "The word Baptist is such a turnoff."[1]

Baptist Temple was facing two problems with its name. Some members believed that the real problem with the name was not "Baptist," but rather "Temple." They felt the word "Temple" conveyed a misleading image of the church. Church member Sue Anderson was among those who thought the name Baptist Temple was kind of bizarre. She was con-

1. Schulte, "Shrinking Flock Examines Its Identity," C01.

3

cerned it conjured up misleading images of tambourines and speaking in tongues.[2]

The idea of changing a church's name became popular in the mid 1990s during the peak of the church growth movement. According to some studies, the general public is apprehensive toward organized religion and traditional denominations. Also, it seems that many of the growing churches in America are either nondenominational or carefully hide their denominational ties.[3]

After debating the possible name change, many in the congregation of Baptist Temple believed the move to be necessary. Similar to other congregations that are experiencing a dwindling attendance, "many Baptist Temple members feel they are at a point where they must either rebrand themselves with a new name, restart as an entirely new church or limp along a few more years before quietly closing their doors."[4]

This was an emotionally charged issue for every member. In its one hundred years, Baptist Temple had survived many setbacks, but it had always found a way to persevere. After discussion and debate from both sides, the Baptist Temple congregation finally took a vote. Thirty-seven people were present for the vote; the church bylaws require a majority vote of two-thirds. In the end, the church compromised and dropped the word "Temple," but kept the word "Baptist" in its name. A majority of twenty-six members voted to change the name to "Commonwealth Baptist Church."[5]

Baptist Temple Church's identity struggle is similar to one facing many congregations in North America. Once the bastion of the local community, churches are now being forced to close down every week. In many cases, these closings have had a devastating impact on the communities around them, especially in urban settings. Yet despite their

2. Ibid.

3. For example, Rick Warren's Saddleback Community Church in Southern California might appear to a first time visitor to be a nondenominational community church. However, upon deeper investigation, one will discover that the church follows the structure and leadership hierarchy of the Southern Baptist Church. Other examples include Robert Schuller's Crystal Cathedral, which is affiliated with the Reformed Church in America, or Adam Hamilton's Church of the Resurrection, and the Ginghamsburg Church—both of which are United Methodist.

4. Schulte, "Shrinking Flock Examines Its Identity," C01.

5. Ibid.

spiritual and social contributions, churches cannot fill their pews or inspire donations to stay in business.

How can the church rebrand its image to address the needs of
the community? Dr. Lovett Weems, director of the Center of Church
Leadership, says the typical local church has two names. It may have an
official name (e.g., Freetown United Methodist Church) emblazoned on
the sign on the front lawn. However, churches may also have a secondary name, given by the local community. It may be "the church that is
only open during weekend services," or "the church that is anti-gay or
anti-abortion." It is important for church leaders to find out what reputation they have in their local community. This unofficial name is even
more important to the church brand than its official name.

LOSING THE BATTLE

The Christian church is experiencing an identity crisis. In a rapidly
changing culture the church has often failed to stay relevant. Once the in-
novator of expression and communication, the church now limps along,
finding ways to keep its doors open, despite any noticeable growth or
evidence of community impact. During the last two centuries, the importance of religion has diminished as society has compartmentalized
each aspect of public life.

The ancient church was once the voice of provocative thought and
expression—the leading entity of language, arts, culture, religion, and
education. It exemplified excellence to the rest of the world. Every aspect
of leadership was taught through the power of the church. The leading
artists, musicians, and writers lived on the premises of the church and
created spectacular works that inspired awe. Nancy Beach, the well-
known pastor for worship at Willow Creek Community Church describes the period when the church of Rome was the center of European
power, "[The church] was the major sponsor of painting and sculptures.
Michelangelo's best-known work was commissioned directly by various
popes, and he was eventually made chief architect of St. Peter's in Rome.
The very idea that the arts in church could be anything less than excellent would have been unthinkable to believers in former centuries."[6] The
church helped communicate the majesty of God. It put into shape, color,
and music the expressions people felt about the Creator.

6. Beach, *An Hour on Sunday,* 148–49.

HOW THE CHURCH LOST TOUCH

During medieval times the church was relevant primarily because religion, politics, and education were all intertwined. The relevancy of each area of life depended on the other discipline. However, today all of that has changed. In contrast to medieval times, education and politics are now assumed as the responsibility of the government. While the church has predominantly led in spiritual development, even this influence is shrinking. The hallmark contributions of the church, such as teaching morality, service to the needy, and finding a higher spiritual source are slowly being outshone by secular entities. Living a moral life was once the indication of a Christian life, but Christians have failed to live up to the high moral calling found in the scriptures.

Recent studies have revealed very few differences between the values and lifestyles of Christians and non-Christians. American theologian and activist Ronald Sider reports that in all instances, from divorce, sexual disobedience, materialism, and physical abuse, Christians are either no different from non-Christians, and in some cases even worse off.[7]

George Barna has remarked on the declining reputation of Christianity. There is a growing sense of disillusionment and disengagement that has settled among 16- to 29-year-olds. Compared to just one decade ago, their trust and interest with the Christian faith has spiraled downward. Barna's study explored twenty images related to Christianity. "Common negative perceptions include that present-day Christianity is judgmental (87 percent), hypocritical (85 percent), old-fashioned (78 percent), and too involved in politics (75 percent)—representing large proportions of young outsiders who attach these negative labels to Christians."[8] As Christians have we become habitual churchgoers who have failed to recognize the importance of the message of Jesus?

ARE WE MAKING A CONTRIBUTION?

With the steady decline in power, influence, and values it becomes necessary to ask: Is Christianity still making a contribution in the world? Despite the decline in morals, Christians still recognize the scripturally based mission to help the needy and the poor. In fact, Christians have

7. See Sider, *The Scandal.*

8. "A New Generation," See www.barna.org. See also, Kinnaman and Lyons, *UnChristian.*

been pioneers in all aspects of mission, often establishing organizations such as the American Red Cross, Compassion International, and Habitat for Humanity, which have led to greater social awareness and commitment.

The contribution churches make in local government are immeasurable. Christian organizations and churches save local government hundreds of billions of dollars by providing social services such as mentoring, counseling, after-school care, soup kitchens, and more. Local governments could never afford the social service burden if not for the investment of local churches.

While the church has made massive contributions to social needs, the demand for volunteers and funding continues to decline. As a result, secular entities are stepping up and serving in place of churches. Celebrities are leveraging their star appeal to bring awareness to various social causes. Icons such as Oprah Winfrey, Bono, and Angelina Jolie are some examples of modern humanitarians who are not aligned with a religious cause, but are making a direct impact.

What has happened? Why are Christians losing ground in being known as service-oriented leaders? In his book *The Barbarian Way*, Erwin McManus suggests that Christians have lost their edge, "Perhaps the tragedy of our time is that such an overwhelming number of us who declare Jesus as Lord have become domesticated—or, if you will—civilized. We have lost the simplicity of the early faith. Beyond that, we have lost the passion and power of that raw, untamed, and primal faith."[9] The passion lost seems to have created a gap between knowing Christ's mission, and acting upon it. This has caused the Christian church to be viewed increasingly like the dinosaur of mission-based revolutions.

WHAT IS THE KINGDOM OF GOD LIKE?

In order to avoid obsolescence, the Christian church must challenge itself to contextualize the gospel in words and images that are understandable to the local culture. The church has struggled to explain God's kingdom in a relevant way. We have attempted to characterize the gospel with language, songs, art, and metaphors from the seventeenth or eighteenth century. However we have failed to characterize the gospel using our own contextual approach.

9. McManus, *The Barbarian Way*, 12.

Jesus was a master of contextualizing the gospel based on his audience. The stories that he told were relevant to the people living in first century Palestine. His use of stories and vivid imagery explained what his Father was like. "All things have been committed to me by my Father. No one knows the Son except the Father, and no one knows the Father except the Son and those to whom the Son chooses to reveal him."[10]

He employed metaphors that were relevant to farmers and merchants in *their* language. In the gospel account of Mark he describes the kingdom of God as a man who "scatters seed on the ground."[11] In Luke, again Jesus describes the kingdom of God "like a mustard seed, which a man took and planted in his garden. It grew and became a tree, and the birds of the air perched in its branches."[12] This language was easily understood. His audience could imagine planting a garden, because it wasn't a hobby for 'green thumbs' in the first century. It was a way of life—sustenance.

Jesus explained the kingdom of God in different ways, depending on the setting and the audience. In Luke's account, Jesus used the example of the mustard seed to describe the kingdom, but in verse twenty he asked a question: "What shall I compare the kingdom of God to?"[13] This is a good example of a fine teacher. An experienced teacher employs different strategies to explain the same concept so the learner can grasp the idea from another angle. Professional educators call this "conceptional learning."

After using the example of mustard seeds, Jesus changed his analogy and used cooking to describe the kingdom of God. He said, "It is like yeast that a woman took and mixed into a large amount of flour until it worked all through the dough."[14] By switching the illustration from agriculture to domestic resources, he clarified His point while using examples that connected with his audience.

10. Matthew 11:27.
11. Mark 4:26.
12. Luke 13:18–19.
13. Luke 13:18–20.
14. Luke 13:20–21.

CONTEXTUALIZING OUR MESSAGE

How can we explain Jesus' message, employing His technique in the secular world we live in? Today's Westerners are living in a culture that has little or no similarities to first century Palestine. Most of us are not farmers. The food we eat comes directly from the local grocery store, packaged and sealed to stay as fresh as possible.

While flour and dough are still ingredients that are essential to cooking, only a fraction of us actually cook from scratch. We cook from boxes and cartons, or go out to dinner. Studying how and where we eat can give great insight into the modern American family. According to one study, Americans are eating out more. "Eating out has changed the dietary habits of Americans. The number of meals eaten away from home has increased from 16 percent in 1977–78 to 29 percent in 1995 . . . Families and people eat out due to more women working outside of the home, more two-salary households, higher incomes, more affordable and convenient fast-food restaurants, increased advertising, and smaller families."[15] Clearly the metaphors used by Jesus were more relevant to his immediate listeners than they would be to Americans today.

Just as in Jesus' day, determining the best possible way to explain God's kingdom is going to change dramatically based on the region in which we live and the defining architecture, cultural nuances, language styles, art, and pop culture. For example, terminology from the world of music can change considerably in just one generation. Imagine saying that the "kingdom of God is like a vinyl album." Most young people have never even seen a real vinyl album. In order to keep up with the new technology permeating our culture, the terminology has changed from album to cassette, to compact disc, to mpeg, to an iTune song.

I once heard Dr. Sathianathan Clarke, a professor at Wesley Theological Seminary, address a group of young clergy about the current state of Christiandom. He said, "You have become CEO's of a mini-institution called Church. And you have been required to preserve it."

To describe a pastor as a CEO and the church as a business may be disturbing to some, but possibly accurate for today's culture. And while it seems permissible for youth ministers, who have been contextualizing the gospel with great success for decades, the attempt to contextualize or change the metaphor in adult settings can be met with great resistance.

15. Stadler and Essa. "The ABC's of Eating Out," Virginia Cooperative Extension, 348–951, June 2001.

While Christians shy away from being associated with business-like models, or the use of business terms, the reality is that our church culture has already adapted business practices and standards. We use words like, "church board" or "board of governors"; we keep agendas and minutes for safe record keeping, and many church leaders look at their congregations as shareholders or investors; we employ models that include vision and mission statements, and develop a set of values—all borrowed from the business world.

It is hard to get away from the current culture we live in. We tend to adopt practices and vocabulary that are common in the secular world. The use of current communication trends should be considered if we are going to connect with a wider audience. Borrowing these practices and terms is not detrimental to the body of Christ, so long as we remain faithful to our theological framework.

As I study the current climate of our culture, I believe a way to best describe the Christian faith in the West is as a brand. The selling or promotion of a product is called branding.

We often associate a brand with a product. A brand may be the kind of soda you drink; it may be the car you drive. Whether it is shoes, cereal, sheets, strollers—it is a brand. A brand is a product that is being sold. The Christian message is a product that has been marketed for the past two thousand years and is in need of a new way to reach the market. The metaphor of branding the Christian faith may teach us how to reach new converts (customers) in the current context of our daily lives.

Branding a message is the very work we are called to do as Christians. Our goal is to carry the product (the meta-narrative of Jesus) to the world. In order to avoid the further decline of the Christian church we must become contextually relevant, by understanding our target audience—discovering what their needs are and how they learn and communicate. We must also identify their dislikes and their concerns. We must understand their values, worldviews, and decision-making processes. Just as missionaries must first learn the language and culture of the land they are living in to successfully share the gospel, so we must learn the cultures that exist in our own context to share the story of Jesus effectively.

2

The Art of Storytelling

Today, whether you're an architect, an evangelist or a cookie marketer, the rules are very different. You win when you manage to make your story coherent.

—Seth Godin, *All Marketers Are Liars*

Branding is the art of storytelling. A brand communicates a story for a product or idea. If a product's image and story yields positive results, the branding process is deemed successful. However, if a brand is unable to move its product, it is considered unsuccessful. Therefore, conveying the brand's story is crucial.

The words "brand" and "branding" are often used interchangeably, but there is a distinction. A "brand" is a product or idea. "Branding," the verb, involves taking a product and making it sell.

Every brand has a story that plays a vital role in economics. Consumers are drawn to compelling narratives. Marketers attempt to sell a story—not the product—and the brand name reminds the consumer of the story behind the product. The earlier consumers identify with a product, the more likely they are to retain lifetime loyalty to the brand. This is why companies spend hundreds of millions of dollars on direct marketing to kids. Some experts suggest that 10 percent of a typical 2-year-old's proper nouns are brand names. An English study estimates that one out of four babies speaks a brand name as his or her first word.[1] Twitchell notes that the basic rule of marketing is to "target the audience just on the entry edge of consumption. Find them before they buy, before they listen to competing brands, and you will get them for life."[2]

1. Twitchell, *Branded Nation*, 2.
2. Ibid., 79.

11

I recently entered an Apple store at a mall and saw 25 children under the age of 10 working at the computers. They were all wearing t-shirts that said, "Apple Camp" with the Apple logo emblazoned on the back. Why would the Apple store offer a free summer camp for kids? If they can get children to become users of their Mac products, they will eventually reap the rewards through brand loyalty for a lifetime. About an hour later as I was walking out the store, I noticed a long line of adults standing outside of the store, with a security officer stationed at the front of the line. At first I thought these were the parents of the summer camp kids, but I was wrong. The adults were waiting in line to purchase to the new iPhone. Twenty years from now the kids from Apple Camp will be standing in line as a new generation of Apple loyalists, waiting to purchase the newest technology.

A MULTITUDE OF BRANDS

Brand names such as Apple, Pepsi, Tide, Playboy, Nike, Starbucks, and Pringles, are all examples of the multiple product choices consumers have. The American grocery store provides another example of the multiple product choices that exist. The average grocery store sits on 44,000 square feet and stocks more than 30,580 items. Most of the products are redundant; there may be fifty different soap products in one aisle. Since most soaps contain the same basic ingredients, how does a particular soap manufacturer distinguish itself as the "best"? The art of branding comes into play at this point, and the ability to distinguish one brand from the others is critical to the economic bottom line.

THE ORIGIN OF BRANDS

Branding has been in the public sphere since the beginning of time. The tree of life and the tree of knowledge of good and evil in Genesis could be considered the two original brands in human history.[3] Every brand must have a story that is compelling, romantic, and larger than life. And every brand must have a nemesis. The trees were polar opposites, each with a unique message. The tree of life offered eternal youth and bliss. The taboo tree of knowledge of good and evil offered unlimited knowledge. Both trees had compelling stories with the power to seduce.

---

3. See Genesis 2:15–17.

Symbology in branding is universal. The word "brand" comes from the old English word, *bieran*, "to burn." As a verb it describes the tempering by high heat. As a noun, a brand is something that is blazoned.[4] A brand is a weapon of sorts—a sword, hardened by heating.

In addition to being a weapon, branding emphasized ownership. It was the mark of the originator. It was used as a stigma (the Latin word for blot or blemish) to signify shame for an unruly slave or servant. Branding was also an early Christian practice. These marks were burned lightly on the believer's skin to indicate a relationship with the church. These marks were reminiscent of Jesus' own nail marks—the stigmata. "The wound's received by Christ on the Cross would miraculously appear on the hands of a true penitent: the secondary stigmata, a brand of elation, not degradation."[5] The most popular use of modern branding is on cattle or other livestock, indicating to whom the animal belongs.

Symbology in branding is ancient. Brand recognition through icons, symbols, words, imagery, and color has played an important role in message transmission. "Symbols express needs, and symbol-making is itself a need. Symbols can carry a positive charge . . . Brand names symbolize benefits."[6] Symbols and pictures have been evident since the Paleolithic era, where stories of family, faith, and war have been portrayed inside cave walls throughout history.

The early Christians adopted the sign of the fish (Icthus) as a secret symbol of the faith. Within the first century, the loaves and fishes art deco was popularized among early Christian communities, often appearing in mosaic form. In the fourth century the cross also became known as a hallmark of the Christian faith. These images, or logos, tell a story about the brand.

HOW BRANDING WORKS

How does branding work? In order to explain this concept, let's use the bottled water industry as an example. Water has been a free commodity since the beginning of time. For decades, the Western world has had clean water available from faucets, both at home and at work. The bottled water industry did not exist in America thirty years ago. However,

4. Twitchell, *Branded Nation*, 17.
5. Ibid.
6. Rivkin and Sutherland, *The Making of a Name*, 131.

as of 2006, Americans spent more money on bottled water than on iPods and movie theater tickets: $15 billion. In 1976, the average American household drank 1.6 gallons of bottled water a year. Last year, according to Beverage Marketing Corporation, Americans drank 28.3 gallons of bottled water. "We drink more bottled water than milk or coffee or beer. Only carbonated soft drinks are more popular than bottled water, at 52.9 gallons annually."[7] Bottled water is undeniably the quintessential example of an expendable income item. How did the bottled water industry create a story so alluring that it would convince Americans to spend money on an item they can get free of charge?

Bottled water exemplifies Americans' thirst for luxury consumerism. The secret behind the industry is a compelling story. Companies created the illusion that tap water might be unclean and was decidedly non-luxurious. Charles Fishman wrote:

> A chilled plastic bottle of water in the convenience-store cooler is the perfect symbol of this moment in American commerce and culture. It acknowledges our demand for instant gratification, our vanity, our token concern for health. Its packaging, and transport depend entirely on cheap fossil fuel. Yes, it's just a bottle of water—modest compared to a Hummer. But when a whole industry grows up around something we don't need—when a whole industry is built on the packaging and the presentation—it's worth asking how that happened, and what the impact is.[8]

The branding of bottled water started when Gustave Leven, chairman of Source Perrier, approached American investor Bruce Nevin. Nevin believed that if the American people could see bottled water as a beverage, like Coke or Pepsi, he could open a market in the United States similar to that of Europe. So how did he create this perception? First, he associated bottled water with exclusivity. In 1977, before Perrier launched its U.S. operations, Nevin flew sixty reporters to France to see "the water source" firsthand. Second, he connected the brand with health. Perrier became an official sponsor of the New York marathon, just as long-distance running was becoming popular. Third, he connected Perrier to celebrity. The company spent $4 million on an advertising campaign featuring Orson Wells. "In 1978, its first full year in the United States,

7. Fishman, "Message in a Bottle," Fast Company, 111–121.
8. Ibid.

Perrier sold $20 million of water."[9] The following year, sales tripled to $60 million. The brand strategy had worked.

The initial success of Perrier also opened a wider market for other water companies. For example, Evian found its own distinctive place in the bottled water business. Americans seemed to prefer the taste of still water, so Evian sold still water, as opposed to the sparkling water offered by Perrier. Evian also packaged its product in a clear bottle to emphasize its purity. It was easier to see the water in Evian's clear bottle, as opposed to Perrier's signature blue bottle. Finally, Evian marketed its product as young and hip. It was not unusual to see advertisements with young, athletic models holding the bottle, or celebrities such as Madonna drinking Evian. Although different than Perrier, Evian was just as successful, if not more, in its use of branding. The bottled water industry exploded with success.

The branding of bottled water was reinforced with mythology. Marketing guru Seth Godin writes, "Marketing is about spreading ideas, and spreading ideas is the single most important output in civilization."[10] The myth the bottled water industry conveyed was that its product was healthier—even better than tap water. This, despite the fact that 24 percent of the bottled water Americans buy is actually tap water that has been repackaged by Coke and Pepsi. Some Americans also maintain that bottled water tastes fresher than regular tap water. However, in blind tests when the water temperature was the same, and the glass was identical, ordinary people could not tell the difference.

The branding story can be found on every water bottle label. The compelling story behind the brand often centers on the remoteness of the water source. Fiji Water boasts that its product comes "from the islands of Fiji." Half of the wholesale cost of Fiji Water goes toward transportation of the product, rather than its actual extraction or bottling. San Pellegrino water boasts of its "bubbling" water source. However, the company extracts its water from "super carbonated volcanic spring waters in Tuscany, then [it is] trucked north and bubbled into Pellegrino."[11]

Perhaps the greatest perpetuation of storytelling comes from Dasani (Coca-Cola), and Aquafina (Pepsi). Both companies use 100 percent tap water, allowing them to have more factories around the United States.

9. Ibid.

10. Godin, *All Marketers Are Liars*, 17.

11. Fishman, "Message in a Bottle," Fast Company, 111–121.

While America has one of the cleanest supplies of drinking water in the modern world, both companies take an extraordinary step through an energy-intensive reverse osmosis filtration process, more powerful than what is used to turn seawater into drinking water. These extraordinary steps enhance the story, and convince consumers that they are drinking "clean, healthy" water.

MARKETING V. BRANDING

Marketing and branding are closely related, although they have different roles. Once a brand has determined its dominant selling idea, the branding strategy will include a marketing and advertising campaign. The marketing campaign falls under the umbrella of the branding strategy.

An effective marketing campaign speaks to the consumer's emotions. Consumers are attracted to the idealization of a product. "Building brands requires building perception—nothing more, nothing less. Creating the perfect perception requires the perfect sensory appeal."[12] A recent Lexus commercial depicted a wealthy couple taking a romantic drive along a rugged coastline until they stopped by a waterfall. As the camera paned inside the vehicle, viewers were struck with the stillness within the sedan's interior, until the window opened and the roar of the waterfall could suddenly be heard.

The commercial was selling the exclusivity of wealth and power. Driving a Lexus will drown out all of the noise (figuratively and literally) so the consumer can focus on what is really important. "It exists in a narrative that is attached by commercial speech—advertising."[13] Most cars feel and drive the same. Researchers indicate that most people—when blindfolded, placed in a car, and driven around—cannot identify the brand, style, or cost of the vehicle. This exemplifies the importance of storytelling.

WHOEVER GETS THERE FIRST . . . STAYS FIRST

Marketing is a race to the top. When a company announces it is the first in its market, it has a stronger chance of staying in first place. Two examples come from presidential politics. During the 2004 election, Senator John Kerry's polls were threatening incumbent President Bush.

12. Lindstrom, *Brand Sense*, 34.
13. Twitchell, *Branded Nation*, 10.

Both had strong credentials up to that point, so something significant was needed to differentiate between the two. Conveniently for Bush, during the final two weeks of the campaign, a series of reports were publicized about Senator Kerry's voting record, which was portrayed as "flip-flopping," and the incredulous *Swift Boat* controversy, which suggested inaccuracies in his Vietnam record. Kerry's campaign vehemently denied the allegations, and worked tirelessly to remind the American public of President Bush's own inconsistent record. But it was too late. The message or the brand had already taken shape. The public had already accepted the Kerry story because he was called into question first.

If a brand's message can stick first, it usually benefits the messenger. Another example of this was exhibited during the first two weeks of January 2008. During the presidential primaries, Senator Hillary Clinton began losing her 10-point lead to Senator Barack Obama. The American people embraced his message of "change." He said on January 3, 2008, "Our time for change has come." Hillary Clinton's message—"experience"—did not resonate with the public as well. Obama's message tugged at the hearts of a hopeful and optimistic public that a better day for America was possible. Suddenly, Clinton modified her message from "experience" to "change" also. But this strategy hurt her because Obama's brand was already linked to the "change" message.

Two brands cannot share the same position. Advertising consultants Al and Laura Ries say it takes time for good products to win the confidence of the consumer. If leaders can stay ahead of the competition, through better products or a better story, they can buy time. "And time is on the side of the leader. Monitoring competition and then matching (or outdoing) their developments is the name of the brand maintenance game today."[14]

DIVERGENCE

Corporations use a concept called divergence to create multiple categories under one brand to open a wider market. This concept is borrowed from Darwin's theory of evolution. Divergence, in that context, referred to the splitting of the ancestral tree to create new branches.[15] For ex-

14. Ries and Ries, *The Origin of Brands*, 33.
15. Ibid., 27.

ample, if Crest were to only sell one type of toothpaste, it would limit its market. However, if the toothpaste can diverge, it will be able to open a wider market. Crest can offer Crest Whitening, Crest Gel, Crest Paste, Crest Kids, etc. These all fall under the brand of Crest, yet the company has widened its appeal to a larger market. Ford Motor Company serves as another example. In 1908 Ford had only one model (the Model-T), color (black), and price. Today there are more than ten different models available with a variety of options.

Divergence has worked well for Ford—stemming market share loss and competing with cheaper foreign cars—and many other companies. However, the brand must retain the support of its shareholders or it could become convoluted. In the 1980s Coca-Cola experienced this phenomenon when it attempted to diverge with New Coke. Consumers were outraged, creating a marketing disaster for the company. Coca-Cola ultimately reintroduced the original product as Coke Classic. Today, the company has more than ten different Coke products, from Coke Classic to Coke Zero.

BRAND LOYALTY

The art of branding requires developing a loyal customer base. "Qualitative data show that improving customer retention has a profound impact on a company's bottom line. Firms that are able to attract and keep the right customers are significantly more profitable than those whose customers defect after a few transactions."[16] In their book *Creating Customer Evangelists,* Ben McConnell and Jackie Huba argue that the key to a successful business is keeping the existing customers happy. Customers must believe in the branding story.[17] If they consistently return, they will become your personal "evangelists" for the product.

Many of the techniques found in the business world can be successfully employed within the church. Targeting children in Christendom is crucial. According to pollster, George Barna, the development of children's spirituality is "typically solidified by the age of nine and those beliefs rarely change to any meaningful degree after age 13."[18] Brand loyalty is a very effective concept that has long-lasting dividends over time.

16. Seybold, *Customers.com*, 53.

17. See McConnell and Huba, *Creating Customer Evangelists.*

18. "Spiritual Progress," see www.barna.org. Also see Barna, Transforming *Children Into Spiritual Champions.*

A company or church should expect its customers or members to be loyal to the brand—enough to become personal evangelists.

Churches should be concerned about retention, just as colleges and universities are dependent on strong retention every semester. Seth Godin writes, "The goal of every marketer is to create a 'purple cow,' a product or experience so remarkable that people feel compelled to talk about it. Remarkable goods and services help ideas spread—not hype-filled advertising."[19] Each brand should have a high percentage of faithful consumers or return shoppers.

19. Godin, *All Marketer Are Liars*, 114.

3

Branding Faith

The easiest thing is to react.
The second easiest thing is to respond.
But the hardest thing is to initiate.

—Seth Godin, *Tribes*

Pastor Jack has just returned from a church growth conference. He is very excited about the new leadership strategies he learned while he was away. "Why didn't I learn this stuff in seminary?" he wonders. His first order of business now is to call a special board of elders meeting to write a new vision and mission statement based on the recommendations of the nationally recognized leadership guru who spoke at the conference. Can you identify with this kind of leader? Do you have a Pastor Jack in your congregation? Are *you* Pastor Jack?

It is easy to be influenced by the latest conference or book on church growth. Some pastors and church leaders easily become "church conference junkies," changing their vision and mission statement every year based on the latest leadership trends they discover. Others attempt to pattern their churches after a successful church they've visited. But before making monumental changes in any church, it is critical to ask two simple questions: "Can we do that?" and "Should we do that?" Church health and growth are dependent on such contextualization. Contextualization is one of the most important elements to consider when evaluating ideas from conferences and books. Just because it is working in Los Angeles doesn't mean it will carry over in Kansas. We all want to see results quickly. Perhaps that is why Pastor Jack and thousands of others like him attempt to clone their churches instead of thoroughly understanding the biblical principles governing healthy congregations.

During the last ten years, we have seen an increase in books and conferences on church leadership. In fact, these days it is hard to sell a book in the Christian market without using the following words in your title: *leadership, irrefutable, principles,* and *growth.* The Christian market has taken its cues from the successful secular leadership branch (think Jack Welch). Why? Because every pastor functions as a mini-CEO of the church he or she is charged to serve!

For decades the church has resisted the controversial idea of using business methodologies in the religious sphere. However, a deeper look reveals that most church hierarchies have borrowed much of their organizational structure from the business sector. But the church is not alone in its borrowing. The business world has also adopted many of its practices from religion.

Today the lines between the church and the business sector continue to be blurred, as both entities influence each other interchangeably. The "leader as shepherd" concept has been widely accepted within the business sector. Blaine McCormick and David Davenport provide a snapshot of a leader in their book *Shepherd Leadership.* Based on Psalm 23, a unique characterization of leadership emerges. "Shepherds do not issue a lot of memos and orders from the corner office; rather, they get out in the field to model and guide."[1] Rather than being portrayed as a simple peasant who lacks direction and goals, the shepherd emerges as one who is quick, mentally agile, and cultivates abundance.

In the midst of busyness, quick decisions, and fast-paced living, a shepherd leader must spend quiet time alone to rejuvenate. The authors refer to this as meditation. "The meditation we propose is not about the emptying of the mind. Rather, we advocate a filling of the mind with a deep, sustained reflection on Psalm 23."[2] Focusing on scripture enables one to commune with God and enter a sacred place of prayer. The leader must balance visioning and administrative duties, while reflecting on the scriptures. These authors have connected with a large segment of secular leaders who are seeking spiritual guidance. Other prominent Christian leaders such as John Maxwell, Laurie Beth Jones, and Ken Blanchard have had extraordinary success writing inspirational leadership books that are making an impact in the public sector.[3]

1. McCormick and Davenport, *Shepherd Leadership,* 7.
2. Ibid., 121.
3. See Maxwell, *Developing the Leader*; Jones, *Jesus CEO*; Blanchard, *Lead Like Jesus.*

During the 1980s religious organizations borrowed many leadership concepts from the business world. Some examples include mission and vision statements. Dr. Lovett Weems, director of the Lewis Center for Church Leadership, argues that the dialogue must take place between both sectors. "Some in the church devalue, or even look with disdain, on administration, management, and leadership as unrelated to 'real ministry.' But today more and more people across denominational lines are coming to see that effective leadership is not only compatible with faithful ministry, it is also essential to the fulfillment of God's calling."[4]

The *New York Times* reported that the Roman Catholic Church started a new curriculum based on management principles at Boston College, a Jesuit institution for its priests and lay workers. "This is not about turning the church into a business, or making sure it's managed like any other institution in corporate America," explained Thomas H. Groome, the theology professor at Boston College who founded the program. "It's about employing good business practices that enhance the mission of the church."[5] The church must be open to new leadership strategies in all areas, including branding, advertising, and strategic implementation. Some critics, however, do not believe the church should take leadership cues from the public sector.

While church attendance and influence has declined, the non-Christian leadership market has skyrocketed. Why? How is the secular market adapting to its audiences? What are some of the success stories taking place in the secular market that the Christian church can adapt?

THE REALITY: CHURCH ATTENDANCE IS A MYTH

With the exception of a few agrarian states such as Ireland and Poland, America has been "the most God-believing and religion-adhering, fundamentalist, and religiously traditional country in Christendom," as well as "the most religiously fecund country" where "more new religions have been born . . . than in any other society."[6] But the American landscape has changed dramatically in recent years, as citizens become less involved in civic organizations, and the American church is now in crisis. On the

---

4. Weems, www.churchleadership.com.

5. Zezima, "A New Emphasis, " *The New York Times,* http://www.nytimes.com/2007/12/15/us/15religion.html.

6. Lipset, "Comment on Luckmann," in *Social Theory,* 185–88. Quoted by Putnam, *Bowling Alone,* 65.

surface America still appears to be overwhelmingly Christian; however, the data suggests it may be in name only. Church attendance rates have dwindled over the last fifty years. As Christians, we take pride in the fact that our country is known as a Christian nation. But are we? Can we legitimately lay claim to that notion just because surveys and polls suggest people still pray and *believe* in God? Isn't there more to being a Christian?

THE CONTRIBUTION RELIGION MAKES

Research suggests that churchgoers are major contributors in their communities. Religiously active men and women acquire important skills such as directing meetings, making speeches, managing disagreements, and growing administratively. Religion also contributes to social networking. People who are actively involved in their faith are more likely to have a greater number of personal contacts in their networks. One survey found regular church attendees had conversations with 40 percent more people on a daily basis.[7] In other words, religion makes a powerful contribution to wider society. This is a fact we need to remind our civic leaders of as we attempt to build relationships within our community. While the influence of religious organizations in the community has been eroding, churches are making a substantial contribution to support the social causes of the elderly, the homeless, and the marginalized. What contribution, if any, are your church members making in your community?

ONE MARKET UNDER GOD

How can people claim to be growing religiously in their personal faith when church attendance is spiraling downwards? During the past half-century, statisticians claimed that 40–50 percent of Americans regularly attended a religious service.

But upon further scrutiny, researchers realized that when asking an individual, "Did you attend church this past week?" a large portion of the respondents, prompted by guilt, were responding according to their personal perception of the "right" answer. So researchers began asking the same question using a softer approach: "List the activities you participated in over the weekend." The answers they received were surprisingly different. Recent data suggests that only 20 percent of Americans

7. Putnam, *Bowling Alone*, 66.

attend a religious service during the weekend. With this evidence, it is obvious that attendance at churches is decreasing.

The overwhelming majority of all Americans believe in God, and three out of four say they believe in immortality.[8] According to pollster George Barna, 84 percent of adults say their religious faith is very important in their lives; 66 percent also say that religion is losing influence in the nation.[9] Another 70 percent claim that their own religious faith is consistently growing deeper.[10] While this seems very encouraging, the research suggests that people are clearly spending less time engaged in church activities and in religious practices such as attending church, praying, studying the Bible, and meditating. There is clearly an inconsistency between what people say they believe and what they do.

PRIVATE FAITH

Religion has become privatized—personal and discreet, with disregard for the larger community. Sociologist George Putnam says, "Privatized religion may be morally compelling and psychologically fulfilling, but it embodies less social capital. More people are 'surfing' from congregation to congregation more frequently, so that while they may still be 'religious,' they are less committed to a particular community of believers."[11] This leads to religious switchers, or what is known in the marketing world as *brand switching*. In a religiously pluralistic society, people are open to new religious expression rather than maintaining the status quo.

Religious options have opened up a whole new market. Religious expansion has only begun to boom in the last century. Religiosity was limited to major brand labels: Hinduism, Judaism, Buddhism, Christianity, and Islam. Even as recently as five hundred years ago, the subcategories within these religions were marginal. Prior to the Reformation, there were about eight major mendicant orders competing for the market in the Church of Rome. However, in the modern era, a conglomeration of religious groups has evolved. Divergence has been witnessed in Christian denominations. Almost every denomination has split in some fashion—creating new sub-brands. For example, according

8. Ibid., 69.

9. "Spiritual Progress," www.barna.org.

10. Ibid.

11. Putnam, *Bowling Alone*, 88.

to Wikipedia.com there are more than 62 Baptist sub-denominations in the United States alone!

Post-secular societies should not be characterized as irreligious. In fact, they are highly spiritual. While these societies are withdrawing from mainstream religions, they are seeking to experiment with new forms of religious expression. As they search for meaning in their lives, they are experimenting with new forms of spiritual engagement. This phenomenon is evidenced in the emergent style worship services that have been transforming Christian worship in the last decade.

A NEW CHRISTIANITY?

The freedom of religion in America has catapulted the birth of new variations in religious groups. According to some estimates, there are more than ten thousand distinct religions around the world, not counting the various unique subsets of each group. Splintering is now the rule, rather than the exception. Twitchell notes that, "Religious pluralism is precisely why the American market is so vibrant while most of the rest of the world dominant religions constrict the flow of competing narratives and enervate the brands."[12] The search for personal meaning is paramount, as people search for a truth *with which they can agree*. We have become consumers—looking for a "truth" that agrees with *our* worldview, rather than being shaped by a greater Truth. This is a Christian fusion of sorts.

Traditional biblical concepts of the Christian church are being compromised. Secular postmodernists are redefining the authority of scripture and the idea of what is holy. "This established and now maturing way of thinking has produced the 'pluralistic' modern society, where there is wide tolerance for any kind of religion but no sure answers relating to values."[13] This trend toward mysticism, meditation, and a fusion of religions, denominations, and sects has blossomed. The decline in church attendance is due in part to the influence of postmodernism's significant characteristic of pluralism. Seekers are in search of meaning, not tradition. They are comfortable with a blend of everything as long as it works for them.

12. Twitchell, *Branded Nation*, 74.
13. Wiklander, "Understanding Secular Minds," *Ministry*, 12–14.

ARE CHURCHES OVERBRANDED?

The conglomeration of religious options may have watered down the market. The church has not been able to differentiate its uniqueness. The American Christian church was once the center of the local community. The city square revolved around the social and religious calendar of the church. However, in recent times, the shopping mall and public school has replaced the traditional role of the church. Additionally, the altar of the television replaced the church altar; the church has lost its ranking.

Economics is dependent on demand. The higher the quantity of a product, the less valuable it is perceived to be. Twitchell argues that the lack of product differentiation of the church has made Protestantism a liability. "The suppliers are redundant and church space is oversupplied."[14] This redundancy can be applied to churches. Are there several churches in your town? Why is there a need for more than one church? If you can't articulate what makes your church unique from the other church down the street or the nonprofit that is making a contribution to the local community, your church may have fallen victim of a phenomenon that I call "overbranding."

To overbrand is to lose your commodity, usually due to oversaturating the market. Overbranding can be observed by campaigns that have overused celebrities, top 40 songs, and popular products. The fickle public will turn on a product as vehemently as they originally embraced it.

Starbucks Company has recently become a victim of overbranding. Starbucks started as a small company with a large story. Just as the bottled water industry created a compelling story to sell its product, Starbucks needed to brand a product that was already available at a low cost. In the 1980s coffee was an ordinary product that most consumers could purchase for 25 cents a cup. If the average cup of coffee sold for only a quarter, what did Starbucks do to compel the average coffee drinker to buy its product for eight to ten times more than the average cup of joe? Howard Schultz, Starbucks CEO, began by asking what would happen if they took the quality coffee bean already attributed to the company and blended it with the lure of a European coffeehouse. Could they rebrand coffee to represent a certain sophistication? By carefully creating a romantic and compelling story that offered an illusion of a rich tasting beverage, the company began to grow. Starbucks sold

14 Twitchell, *Branded Nation*, 65.

an experience instead of a mere product. The Starbucks coffeehouses created a warm, inviting atmosphere where customers were encouraged to sit for hours—a living room setting—without having to clean up afterward. Starbucks became an intermediary safe zone. Or as sociologist Ray Oldenburg says, a "third place," a location other than home or work that is a "neutral, safe, public gathering spot."[15] I have discovered that many of my parishioners would rather meet for pastoral counseling or a "home visit" at the local coffeehouse, than take on the pressure of cleaning up and entertaining their pastor in their own homes.

Starbucks created the living room format, which evoked a feeling of comfort, unlike running into the local 7-Eleven to pick up a "cup of joe" and rushing off. The company recreated the atmosphere of the local neighborhood bar, with its own variation of a bartender, called a *barista*. Starbucks also introduced Americans to a new vocabulary: *venti, chai, Frappuccino,*™ and other blended concoctions that are cemented in the American consciousness.

The chain immediately became a popular social destination. It became a leader in customer service and product customization. It was not unusual for each customer to order a very different drink, based on his or her personal preference: *"Tall, skim caramel macchiato with light whipped cream, and extra caramel on top. And please double cup it."* While employee wages remained nominal, Starbucks became an international leader in employee benefits—offering flexible schedules, health insurance, and other benefits. Each employee was considered a "partner" instead of a worker. Starbucks employees had an 82 percent job-satisfaction rating, according to a Hewitt Associates Starbucks Partner View Survey, compared to 50 percent, the industry standard in 2007.[16] The company was on the fast track in worldwide sales.

> Healthy sales force = happy customers.
> Healthy membership = growing church.

The coffee giant managed to diversify by offering a wide range of products other than coffee, such as games, mugs, food products, and coffee-related merchandise. The industry phrase for these kinds of items

15. O'Rourke, "Venti Capitalists," The New York Times, http://www.nytimes.com/2007/12/16/books/review/O-Rourke-t.html?pagewanted=1&_r=1&sq=ORourke%20Venti%20Capitalists&st=cse&scp=1.

16. Michelli, *The Starbucks Experience*, 9.

is "Grab and Go." Have you ever been standing in line at a Starbucks or Panera Bread, and decided to just grab what's on display, such as a muffin or a bottled drink? Grab and Go items often make up 30 percent of the sales for small stores. In an increasingly diverse society, having many options for people to choose from is paramount.

TAKING ON THE GLOBAL MARKET

In October 2004, Starbucks brokered a deal with XM satellite radio. It would play music over the XM satellite radio waves, introducing customers to old and new artists. The CDs of the featured artists would be available for sale in the coffeehouse.

Starbucks was not only competing with other coffeehouses, it was now competing with big-box record stores. In September 2004, Madeleine Peyroux's album, *Careless Love* was released nationally. It was introduced to Starbucks customers six months later. After one week, the song catapulted to No. 81 on the Billboard chart— her highest chart ranking at the time. Starbucks venues sold more than twice as many of her albums than traditional retailers did during that week.[17]

In 2007 Starbucks began allowing customers to immediately download a song to their computer or mobile device, for a small fee of 99 cents per song. "For the customer it's instant gratification," said Ken Lombard, president of Starbucks Entertainment. "You'll hear the song, be able to identify what it is and download to the device."[18] It seemed the company was not slowing down at all.

THE RISE AND FALL

The company also had high ambitions for U.S. and international growth. In 1980, during a shareholders meeting, Howard Schultz disclosed his vision to open 11,000 stores worldwide. There were many skeptics who could not imagine that consumers outside of Seattle would pay a high cost for a cup of coffee.

The power of the Starbucks brand has also benefited the broader coffeehouse industry. In 1989, there were only 585 coffeehouses in

---

17. Daniels, "Coffee Maker," *Fast Company*, 25.

18. Richtel, "At Starbucks," *The New York Times*, http://www.nytimes.com/2007 /10/01/technology/01impulse.html?scp=1&sq=Richtel+Starbucks&st=nyt.

America. Today, there are more than 24,000, with 57 percent being "mom and pop" type establishments.

Despite its initial success, the over-identification of the company created backlash, leading to overbranding. Many critics have said the company grew too quickly. Its long-range goal was to open 40,000 stores worldwide, and Starbucks was adding six new stores per day. However, the company's expansion was moving faster than its demand; it was saturating the market.

By the late 1990s Starbucks was beginning to lose its global influence and saw its stocks plummet by 43 percent. The company experienced its steepest annual decline since it went public in 1992.[19] In 2006, an infamous internal memo by Shultz, now the company chairman, was leaked in which he criticized the rampant growth and feared "a watering down of the Starbuck's experience."[20] The watering down or overbranding of the product had begun.

As a worldwide global leader in the industry, the company became the target of controversy. The company was not seen as a leader in the Fair Trade movement. While Starbucks was the largest international purveyor of Fair Trade coffee—18 million pounds in 2006—it was viewed as a latecomer in this arena. Despite its perceived domination in the industry, Starbucks buys a little more than 2 percent of the world's coffee.[21] Starbucks' positive image of humanitarian involvement in the popular movement to help farmers in developing nations with their small businesses may have also come too late.

The overbranding of Starbucks led to the questioning of the brand. Many critics began asking if the company's coffee was really worth its cost. Some accused it of purposefully brewing a bitter house blend to encourage its customers to purchase higher priced blended specialty drinks. In recent years, global giant McDonald's Corporation took on Starbucks in

19. "Shares tumble," *Chicago Tribune,* http://pqasb.pqarchiver.com/chicagotribune /access/1400204711.html?dids=1400204711:1400204711&FMT=CITE&FMTS=CITE :FT&type=current&date=Dec+18%2C+2007&author=Anonymous&pub=Chicago+Tr ibune&edition=&startpage=2&desc=Shares+tumble+5%25+after+downgrade.

20. Gillespie, "Starbucks Replaces CEO," *The Huffington Post,* http://www.huffington post.com/huff-wires/20080108/starbucks-ceo/.

21. O'Rourke, "Venti Capitalists," *The New York Times,* http://www.nytimes.com /2007/12/16/books/review/O-Rourke-t.html?pagewanted=1&_r=1&sq=ORourke%20 Venti%20Capitalists&st=cse&scp=1.

a *Consumer Reports* coffee taste test and won![22] In addition, McDonald's launched plans to take on the world's largest coffee chain by offering specialty coffee drinks in almost all of its 14,000 U.S. stores.

Finally, recent months have seen the American economy slowing down, possibly dipping into a recession. Discretionary spending became limited due to the weak American dollar, high gas and propane prices, and collapsing mortgages. People have begun restricting their spending on luxury items such as coffee.

Starbucks has reported that it will slow its growth in the United States and focus on its international endeavors. The company will close 600 of its low-performing stores.[23] It will also concentrate on introducing new products, store designs, and improving training for baristas.[24] The company must revive its brand image by redeveloping its story.

The future of Starbucks will depend on its ability to rebrand. The Starbucks story of "romantic European allure" was lost. It fell into a similar trap as the American Protestant Church, by failing to keep its dominant selling idea—the vital story—as the central focus of the brand. Can the corporate giant redefine its story into something that is believable, wooing its customers back? Only time will tell.

The church can learn a lesson from Starbucks. Is it possible that churches have saturated the market in the American landscape? Perhaps the overbranding of churches has led to a convoluted message.

The Christian faith has an extraordinary chance to rebrand its story. There is no better time to share this life-changing story than now! As the world flattens and viral media explodes with new forms of communicating to a global audience, this is the time to seize the opportunity. Marketing guru Seth Godin says in his book *Tribes*, "The market wants you to be remarkable. The most important tribes [or churches] are bored with yesterday and demand tomorrow. Most of all, the market has demonstrated that ideas that spread win, and the ideas that are spreading are the remarkable ones."[25] The Christian narrative is a *remarkable* one. The story has already been told, now we need to retell it in a way that will stick.

22. "Ailing Starbucks," *The Washington Post*, sec. D03.

23. Unlike McDonald's, Starbucks does not franchise its stores. It is solely responsible for the output of each store.

24. Gillespie, "Starbucks Replaces CEO," *The Huffington Post*, http://www.huffington post.com/huff-wires/20080108/starbucks-ceo/.

25. Godin, *Tribes*, Kindle edition.

4

Rebranding: How It Works

We have created a phenomenal subculture with our own media, enter-
tainment, educational system, and political hierarchy so that we have the
sense that we're doing a lot. But what we've really done is created a ghetto
that is easily dismissed by the rest of society.

—BOB BRINER, *ROARING LAMBS*[1]

REBRANDING: A CASE STUDY

The Starbucks predicament is similar to what the Protestant church has
been experiencing. The church has lost its influence and failed to capture
its own consumers. Consumers, or church members, are not supporting
the business of religion as they once did. They have switched brands or
completely stopped attending.

The secularization of America has already begun. A recent study by
the Pew Research Center for the People and the Press found that about a
third of all Americans have left the religion they grew up in. A different
study found that "In 2008, Christians comprised 76 percent of U.S. adults,
compared to about 77 percent in 2001 and about 86 percent in 1990.
Over the last seven years, mainline Protestants dropped from just over
17 percent to 12.9 percent of the population."[2] Researchers said the dwindling ranks of mainline Protestants—including Methodists, Lutherans,
and Episcopalians—largely explains the shift toward secularization.

The idea that America is a "Christian nation" has been eroding year
after year. In 2008, The Program of Public Values at Trinity College in

1. Briner, Roaring Lambs, 31.

2. http://www.newsvine.com/_news/2009/03/09/2521636-more-americans-say
-they-have-no-religion.

31

Hartford, Connecticut surveyed 54,461 English and Spanish-speaking adults on how religion influences or impacts their lives. The study found traditional organized religion playing less of a role in many lives. Thirty percent of married couples did not have a religious wedding ceremony and 27 percent of respondents said they did not want a religious funeral.[3]

As Christian leaders, we must face the fact that we are losing the battle in sharing the life-changing story of Jesus! Are we in a rut, doing the same things—writing the same books, conducting the same evangelistic series, preaching the same sermons, singing the same songs? Bob Briner writes: "We have created a phenomenal subculture with our own media, entertainment, educational system, and political hierarchy so that we have the sense that we're doing a lot. But what we've really done is created a ghetto that is easily dismissed by the rest of society."[4] Briner's statement is a strong indictment of how the church has created a subculture that is only suitable for Christians.

What are we doing wrong? If there is nothing wrong with the story, then perhaps there is something faulty about the way we are telling it. We need to rebrand the *story* in a way that will be contextually relevant to our audience. To rebrand the church we must determine why people are leaving and why they are no longer interested in church. Second, we must understand who our target audience is, and develop a strategy that will reach the felt needs of the consumer (also known in some circles as seekers, unchurched, or dischurched). In this chapter, I will briefly share a turnaround story from the business sector and outline principles we can learn from it.

UNDERSTANDING WHO YOUR TARGET AUDIENCE IS

It is hard to imagine how the great shoe company, Nike, could ever make marketing mistakes. As the leader of the pack, Nike has continually dominated and crushed its competition with enormous success. It may surprise you to know that Nike *almost* made a fatal error that could have cost hundreds of millions of dollars and ended its standing as the number one sports apparel company in the world.

The company was a latecomer in the emerging women's market.[5] Although the Oregon-based company led in sales of more than $1.7 bil-

3. See the 2008 American Religious Identification Study.

4. Briner, Roaring Lambs, 31.

5. Cole, "The Year That Girls Ruled," *Journal of Sports & Social Issues*, 1, 3.

lion worth of shoes and apparel, in 1990 it was slow to recognize the growing market for women's athletic apparel.[6] Nike had built a strong reputation over decades, earning the trust and recognition of men worldwide. However, the company needed to develop a winning strategy to compete against other brands that had already broken into the female market. How could the company rebrand its image without losing its loyal male consumers? Once Nike recognized the potential market that was opening up, it developed an aggressive campaign, targeting female consumers in the race to capture the growing field. In doing so, Nike faced a monumental challenge of rebranding.

WHO'S MISSING FROM YOUR AUDIENCE?

While Nike's reaction was slow, it still recognized that a major constituency was missing from its market: women. In rebranding your church, one of the hardest questions your congregation must ask is: "Who is missing?" While homogeneity is often comfortable and "safe," for your members, does your congregation represent the diversity found in the kingdom of God? Lovett Weems, executive director of the Center for Church Leadership, has often remarked that a leader must stand above the crowd and recognize who is missing.

Who are the people missing in your congregation? Are they teenagers? Are they first generation immigrants? Are they gays and lesbians who no longer feel the love of the Christian faith? What are you willing to do to receive these missing groups into your church? What changes will be required to accommodate them?[7]

WHAT DOES THE RESEARCH SAY?

Successful organizations study their audience. They are interested in learning about their changing lifestyle habits, such as shopping, education, socioeconomic levels, average commute times, etc. Why do organizations spend millions of dollars studying their consumer base? It is because they are trying to be contextually relevant—to meet the needs of their target audience. How would demographic research of your sur-

6. Schwartz, "Stalking the Youth Market," *Newsweek*, 34.

7. Many churches confuse the word "hospitality" for church luncheons or potlucks, or having a friendly greeter opening the door for weekend services. Biblical hospitality requires much greater principles that affect both the stranger and the host. For a helpful understanding of biblical hospitality, read Genesis 18, and Oden, *God's Welcome*.

rounding community change the way you preached, or how would it shape your small group ministry or outreach ministry?

By conducting its own research, Nike discovered that women in the 1990s had greater purchasing power and expendable income than was believed. In fact women had a stronger influence on personal home finances than in the previous decade. A 1998 study published in *Modern Healthcare* revealed that a large percentage of women make the financial health care decisions in their homes. "Women make 64 percent to 80 percent of the health care decisions in their households, according to several sources. What's more, 80 percent of drugstore purchases and 60 percent of all doctor visits are made by women."[8] *This was an untapped market.*

FAILURE TO CAPTURE THE WOMEN'S MARKET

During the early 1990s, when the emerging women's market exploded, most corporations were spending their marketing budget and research to target men. However, several key developments arose. Lifetime Television for Women, Oxygen Channel, and female-dominated sports such as the Women's National Basketball Association (WNBA) are just a few examples of the developments that altered the landscape for a neo-feminist movement.

Market researchers failed at first to recognize this promising new arena. At the time corporations such as Nike believed that it was only a temporary trend that would quickly pass.[9] They were mistaken.

By the time Christian leaders began commenting on the post-modern influence on our culture, monumental shifts had already taken place.[10] The church suddenly woke up to a new era that had been evolving for decades. Phil Cooke writes, "The culture will always be shifting, and it will always be with us."[11] While we were still doing "church" as if it were 1952, the world shifted. The way we engage popular culture, even the methodology of how the mind absorbs information due to the effect of media, has completely transformed the world.

By following trends and demographic statistics, churches and religious organizations can better understand the evolving culture. It may

---

8. Ngeo, "The First Gatekeeper," *Modern Healthcare*, 34.
9. Cole, "The Year That Girls Ruled," *Journal of Sports & Social Issues*, 3.
10. See Grenz, *A Primer on Postmodernism*.
11. Cooke, *The Last TV Evangelist*, 38.

be surprising that many mega-churches already employ professional research companies to help them understand the changing culture and demographics surrounding their churches—just like Nike. A 2005 *Washington Post* article highlights this phenomenon:"[C]ompanies in this field [consultancies] have been helping pastors incorporate multimedia technologies into Sunday services and use sophisticated marketing techniques to draw larger crowds."[12]

COURAGEOUS LEADERSHIP

One of the first companies to recognize the transition in women's financial power was Sears. Sears and Roebuck traditionally targeted its marketing campaigns to men, featuring Home and Garden accessories such as lawnmowers, and its trademark Craftsman Tool Set. But once the company recognized the new power of women, it revamped its corporate image, revealing the "Softer Side of Sears" in its advertising.

After realizing its failure to lead the industry in female-driven merchandise, Nike buried itself in research, using outside polling agencies such as Rand Youth Poll and Teen Research Unlimited. The company found that young teen girls had a proclivity to using their expendable income on clothing, in contrast to boys in the same age group. According to the *Journal of Sports and Social Issues*, "Teen girls are far greater impulse buyers than young men, visit stores more often, are more socially involved, have less sales resistance, and have a high-fashion and fad consciousness, all of which contribute to their spending propensity."[13] Nike took a courageous leadership leap to first study its potential consumers in order to best meet their needs.

If your church is going to successfully rebrand, it will require courageous leadership as well. Many of our church leaders today are not *leading*; rather, they are *managing* congregations (in fact, they are doing an exemplary job at managing). Management means to follow the status quo; to keep doing what is expected. Seth Godin writes, "We choose not to be remarkable because we're worried about criticism. We hesitate to create innovative movies, launch new human resource initiatives, design a menu that makes diners take notice, or give an audacious sermon because we're worried, deep down, that someone will hate it and call us on it."[14]

12. Cho, "The business of filling pews, " C1. Quoted in Einstein, *Brands of Faith*, 61.

13. Ibid.

14. Godin, *Tribes*, 46.

What is preventing you from taking a courageous leadership step? Is it fear of failure? Is it criticism? Is it the fear of losing what is comfortable?

STRATEGY WITHOUT LOSING INTEGRITY

As Nike prepared to launch its women's marketing campaign, it had to seriously consider how women would be portrayed. Although it wanted to accurately portray female athletes as being just as serious as their male counterparts, the company faced the difficult decision of whether it should soften its image as Sears and Roebuck had done to reach a wider market.

At that time, the popularity of physically appealing athletes such as Anna Kournikova, Sheryl Swoopes, and Mia Hamm tempted companies to blur the lines of athletic greatness and sexual appeal. "One of the beauties of being a woman today is that you can be a lot of different things," says Jackie Thomas, the director of women's marketing at Nike, who also says she believes that "glamour is one of the many options that should be afforded to female athletes."[15] The company combined the sexuality of women while representing their athleticism.

Supporting this statement was a surge in women's periodicals, journals, and newspapers at the time, which led to a "rebranding" of women, captured in the advertising pages of contemporary magazines such as *Cosmopolitan* and *Glamour*. "The woman is not shown leaning on a man or surrounded by other women—depictions which might imply that she requires the company of others to legitimate her identity."[16] She is now understood to possess a unique spirit that suggests empowerment, strength, and individuality. "The lone woman embodies, physically and figuratively, the cultural and historical shift from the home to the outside world."[17] The rebranding campaign not only revolutionized the traditional ideal of a woman for Nike, but also reshaped the image of women in our society as a whole!

NIKE DEVELOPS AN IDEOLOGICAL CAMPAIGN

Women were given permission to be both soft and strong. "Sexy" was now associated with strength, power, and determination. With an explosion of women's sports in the 21st century and an elevated interest in fe-

15. When it Comes to Marketing Females," *New York Times*, C2.
16. Ibid.
17. Ibid.

male sports celebrities, Nike seized the opportunity to launch a spirited marketing campaign.

According to a November 2000 Zogby Poll, the Nike brand was on the top of the list of Americans' favorite athletic footwear.[18] Because of Nike's remarkable reputation as a sports authority, catching up to its competition was not hard to do. Nike followed its usual course by using powerful tools such as celebrity endorsement, vivid imagery, and socially conscious ideology. In 2001, the marketing offensive also included six new television spots, five print advertisements, an Internet site and a new women's fitness magazine called *Nike Goddess*.[19]

IDEOLOGICAL CAMPAIGN OR PROPHETIC IMAGINATION?

In order to brand successfully, companies must embed an accurate depiction of the product within the advertising. However they must also carefully guide the consumer to envision the future. Borrowing from Walter Brueggemann, leaders must have a *prophetic imagination*.[20] To rebrand you must offer your target audience (and your existing congregation) a "preferred altered reality." You must describe who you want to be, not who you already are . . . just as Nike did with women. Courageous leaders will cast a bold vision, describing what the church can look like, instead of what the church is.

Rebranding requires envisioning the possibilities. In 2004 I moved from a forward-thinking congregation that was making a significant impact in its community to the New Hope Church in Maryland. New Hope was a progressive congregation—or at least they thought they were—as long as they stayed within safe boundaries.

HOW SYMBOLS PREPARE YOUR AUDIENCE

To reach your community you must be prepared to allow *anybody* in. That means being ready to get dirty and be dirty. It means putting yourself at risk. It means worshipping and sharing your life with people you

18. Reuter/Zogby, November 6, 2000. This national poll of 1,264 showed that Nike was the most preferred shoe company (33 percent), followed by Reebok (14 percent), Adidas (8.4 percent), New Balance (7 percent), and Converse (3.1 percent).

19. "Women Athletes," *Dallas Morning News*, 1.

20. I don't want to give the impression that Walter Brueggemann's book is on the subject of branding, however in many ways it is. See Brueggemann, *The Prophetic Imagination*.

would normally avoid in everyday encounters. Biblical hospitality means you are willing to make accommodations so *others* will feel accepted.

After deciding who our target audience would be at New Hope Church, we also tried to think of ways to lower the stress levels for these individuals when they visited our church for the first time. One of the specific changes we made was to add ashtrays at each of the entrances of the church. As you can imagine, some people objected.

What are you thinking? We don't want smokers near our church! These people will corrupt our kids. This will change our church.

What I didn't realize was that this simple symbol—an ashtray—would create an immense cultural change. In fact, the ashtray became symbolic of the impending changes in New Hope's culture.

Change didn't happen overnight. At first the ashtrays were a source of contention for many of the longtime saints. Some of the church leaders wanted to convene a special elders meeting to discuss my lack of judgment. On several occasions the ashtrays went missing—yes, missing—and I was forced to hunt them down and return them to the entrances prior to the weekend services.

New Hope Church has evolved since then. No, there are not hundreds of people smoking outside our doors. However, five years later, there are more unchurched people who come to our church with cigarettes hanging from their lips, which they drop in the ashtrays before stepping through the doors for the service. While the ashtrays are a "hospitable gesture" for the smoking consumer, they symbolize something larger—a changing climate among longtime church members. The ashtrays prepared the congregation to embrace people who are different. Every week, they provide a physical reminder of what it means to be a loving and embracing church.

Symbols are important. They are a tactile representation of the preferred altered reality. Symbols send a subtle message to your congregation that you are serious about the "prophetic imagination"—and they better prepare for it.

THE YEAR THAT GIRLS RULED

Nike seized the opportunity created by the changing times by launching its substantial advertising campaign for women at a time when America's interest in women's sports was at a heightened level, as demonstrated by the unprecedented media coverage of women's soccer and the WMBA.

What are the opportunities your church could be seizing right now? What are the buzzwords you keep hearing over and over? Buzz is what your consumers are suddenly interested in. The Kashi brand has created enormous buzz by creating a corporate identity around "organic products." I love Kashi products. But to be honest, it isn't the taste or the health index printed on the side of the box (I urge you to compare the "health" information of a Kashi cereal with your regular morning cereal. You may be surprised by the similarities rather than the differences). Mara Einstein says, "Branding is about making meaning—taking the individual aspects of a product and turning them into more than the sum of its parts. It is about giving consumers something to think or feel about a product or service beyond its physical attributes. *It's about fulfilling a need; providing what marketers call the benefit.*"[21] Kashi is selling a story, more than a product. I love their story. In fact, I have been drawn in as one of their followers, because I inherently support their philosophy of healthy living.

During the first several months of 2009, the evangelical world was in a tizzy over a short article in the *New York Times* by Paul Vitello, titled "Bad Times Draw Bigger Crowds to Churches."[22] The story claimed that churches were experiencing "a burst of new interest that they find themselves contending with powerful conflicting emotions . . . Bad times are good for evangelical churches."[23] It is true. A University of Texas study shows that members are more likely to return to church during hard economic times. These are the kinds of cultural shifts that we should be conscious of. As we track the cultural shifts, we will be better equipped to seize the opportunity to rebrand our message.

Branding is effective when a consistent brand manager oversees the product for a long period. Nike's aggressive rebranding campaign

21. Einstein, *Brands of Faith*, 70. Italics added for emphasis.

22. Vitello, "Bad Times," *New York Times*, A1.

23. While this story created enormous buzz, it was sharply misrepresented. Based on a University of Texas study, many news articles concluded that church attendance was on the rise because of a high volume of unchurched attendance. Paul Vitello quoted a largely unknown, unpublished study by David Beckworth, professor of economics, who used the total annual membership of twenty-four Protestant denominations. While this may seem subtle, the growth described during hard economic times was based on the church membership attendance. In other words, members tend to return to their roots during difficult times. See http://www.christianitytoday.com/ct/2009 /januaryweb-only/153-51.0.html and http://cotent.usatoday.com/communities/religion /post/2009/03/64013951/1?csp=34.

was successful in part due to its founder Phil Knight's recognition of the changing market. Nike's ability to break into the women's market demonstrates its ability to develop a winning strategy without losing its loyal consumers. The Protestant church could learn valuable lessons from Nike on how to rebrand its story. Who oversees the consistent image or message of your church? Who protects your church from pastors who continually change their tune based on the last conference they attended or book they read?

THE CHALLENGES OF RELIGIOUS BRANDING

The challenge with branding in the religious sphere is the temptation to water down the original message to reach a wider audience. Branding in the business sector allows an altered narrative, even if it is untrue.

> Popeye the Sailor says you will be stronger if you eat spinach.
> Disney is the happiest place on earth!
> Captain Crunch is a cool pirate who will lead you to a new treasure.

Are any of these true? Of course not (well, except for Disney!). The use of mythology, folklore, mystical creations, and other creative forms of storytelling is widely accepted in the secular realm. Churches don't have that luxury. We already have a true story that many millions believe to be an untrue folktale.

When Toyota Motor Company was trying to break into the urban twenty-something demographics, it needed to change its image by creating an alter ego. Toyota had already created a brand: safe, dependable, no risk, family-type sedans (think Camry). The Toyota Scion entered the market as a tough, no-nonsense vehicle that would connect with the young consumers the company was seeking. *USA Today* writer, James R. Healey wrote, "Toyota's small, youth-oriented Scion xB is everything its corporate cousin Scion xA is not: ugly, tinny, roomy and frisky."[24] The company still used the same Toyota parts and manufacturing plants, and the car was still a Toyota. However, it created a new story of sleek speed and testosterone. Toyota does not have the same ethical or moral obligations to its story as the Christian church does. It can alter or even falsify its image to reach a wider consumer base. The church cannot.

24. Healey, "It's Hip," *USA Today*, http://www.usatoday.com/money/autos/reviews/healey/2004-03-11-scion-xb_x.htm.

The church already has a meta-narrative called the gospel. While some have said it is the most compelling, transforming story in the history of mankind, why isn't it yielding higher dividends? Does the brand narrative need to be revised?

The church has modified the gospel story based on an ever-changing interpretation of scripture. This is demonstrated by the wide diversity of denominations, sects, and cults. It also highlights the immense challenge of brand maintenance when there is no single executive to manage the story. This leads to continually evolving storylines that change based on the consumer's expectations or desires.

When Christians cannot agree on fundamental theological beliefs, the brand is put at risk. Take for instance a televised debate on ABC's *Nightline* show. On March 26, 2009, host Dan Harris gathered four religious leaders to debate the existence of the devil. The *Face-off* was hosted at Mars Hill Church in Seattle. The panel included lead pastor Mark Driscoll; Annie Lobert, a former prostitute who now runs an organization called "Hookers for Jesus" that ministers to sex workers; Dr. Deepak Chopra, the spiritual New Age guru; and Bishop Carlton Pearson who has publicly denounced the existence of Satan.

Chopra, the author of dozens of bestselling books and the leader of millions of disciples, eloquently explained why healthy people don't need Satan as a justification, "My position is that we have a huge problem with what people call evil in the world and they need a good rational explanation and not an irrational mythical explanation."[25]

Supporting Chopra's arguments was former pastor, Carlton Pearson, who claimed to have cast out demons earlier in his ministry. "I'm from four generations of demon caster-outers," Pearson countered. "I had tremendous faith in the devil and his power and his omnipresence . . . I have reassessed all of that and I think that the best way to get people free is to get them to stop believing so much in this hairy, horny, freaky, scary, omnipresent entity and it will not manifest the way we have believed it to. And that will bring an element of peace."[26] Spiritual and Christian leaders are compromising the theological doctrine concerning good and evil. While 70 percent of Americans believe in the existence of Satan, many church leaders are bringing doubt to the subject. If the

25. Harris, "Tempers Flare," www.abcnews.go.com.
26. Ibid.

church cannot agree on basic fundamental truths, how in the world will we ever be perceived to have any sense of integrity?

John MacArthur suggests that the church's vacillating message has led to confusion, "The church's influence is actually diminishing. Our message is becoming confused—and is confusing. We are not speaking the truth plainly for the world to hear the message."[27]

MacArthur suggests that society has moved out of the age of exposition and into the age of sound bites. The church must face the reality that its consumers have shortened attention spans for everything, including religious teachings. The popularity of prosperity messages has raised the question of whether the pastor as prophet should proclaim what people want to hear or remain faithful to the gospel message, even when it is not popular to be the "voice in the wilderness." Popular religious pollster George Barna has suggested that reaching the masses may require the *audience* to set the tone of the message:

> It is . . . critical that we keep in mind a fundamental principle of Christian communication: the audience, not the message, is sovereign. If our advertising is going to stop people in the midst of hectic schedules and cause them to think about what we're saying, *our message has to be adapted to the needs of the audience.* When we produce advertising that is based on the take-it-or-leave-it proposition, rather than on a sensitivity and response to people's needs, people will invariably reject our message."[28]

Many churches have grown substantially by marketing their message to the felt needs of their consumers. Felt needs-based evangelism has been perceived by its critics as an attempt to find the lowest common denominator for doing Christian ministry. Willow Creek Community Church, in South Barrington, Illinois, has grown to more than twenty thousand in attendance by targeting the felt needs of the community. Bill Hybels, founder and lead pastor, has been widely criticized for watering down the gospel message to attract large crowds.

Hundreds of books promise to unlock the "secret" to growing a successful church. You can spend tens of thousands of dollars on direct marketing pieces, a top-of-the-line Web site, and award winning graphic design, but these are all secondary. While marketing and advertising are

27. MacArthur, "A Challenge," 7–15.

28. Barna, *Marketing the Church,* 145 (italics added for emphasis). Quoted by MacArthur in "A Challenge," 7–15.

important elements to branding, they are not the keys to growing your church. The only thing that will grow a healthy, successful church is changed lives. That is the bottom line. Once people are transformed by the power of the Holy Spirit and the faithfulness of your congregation will you finally have a story or a testimony to share with the outside world.

5

Paul's Branding Strategy

THE APOSTLE PAUL WAS enormously gifted in communicating his message to a diverse audience. In spite of numerous obstacles, he developed a brand that spread throughout the known world. His success was based largely on his ability to adapt to the unique audiences he addressed.

Paul's life and writings have been scrutinized over the last two millennia to prove a multitude of points and theological differences. While some consider him to be an excellent teacher, evangelist, theologian, and writer, others have faulted his writings and missionary endeavors as misogynistic, homophobic, and unbalanced. Yet Paul's approach can be understood in the context of his audience; his message was largely shaped by the social and environmental climate of his day. Despite conflicting viewpoints, Paul provides a valuable example of how the church should rebrand itself in our modern day.

PAUL'S MULTICULTURAL EDGE

Paul's personal background enabled him to reach a worldwide audience. He was born Saul, around the same time as Jesus—a Jew of the Dispersion. "He came from the 'free' (that is to say self-governing and privileged) Greek city of Tarsus, a region of southeastern Asia Minor which was part of the Roman province of Syria-Cilicia. Paul claimed descent from the Jewish tribe of Benjamin and belonged to a family of strict Pharisees."[1]

He "was an urbanite and a cosmopolitan, moving easily throughout the Greco-Roman world. He could probably speak Aramaic (or Hebrew,

1. Grant, *Saint Paul*, 13.

or both), and he may have known Latin, but his main tongue was one of the greatest international languages of all time, *koine* (common) Greek."[2] His multilingualism, his deep understanding of Hellenistic culture and thought, his religious zeal,[3] and his training under the leading Pharisee of the day, Gamaliel,[4] demonstrate his expansive knowledge.[5]

CONVERGING PAUL'S PERSUASIVE MESSAGE

One of the most important concepts in marketing today is convergence. Marketers are looking for "partners" to push a product or message. Developers have responded to the customized desires of their consumers and created many converged products. The handheld PDA is a good example of a converged brand: it is a mix between a personal computer and cell phone. A two-in-one shampoo and conditioner is another simple example. The product is not necessarily better, but it is more convenient.

Convergence is also popular within ideological, theological, and political circles. Politicians have branded their message by converging their persona: "Moderate Democratic," "Compassionate Republican"— buzzwords borrowed from the other side. Al and Laura Ries say, "Taking an existing technology and applying it to a narrow market segment is the surest way to build a brand."[6] Paul also converged his message by blending both Jewish and Greco-Roman cultures. Paul used letter writing as his technology to advance his message. His multicultural background and multilingual ability enabled him to take the fledging Christianity and craft his own gospel brand.

Paul's ability to move in and out of both Jewish and Gentile settings gave him the ability to understand and communicate within both cultures. "Thus Paul possessed the remarkable qualification of belonging to three different worlds: Jewish, Greek, and Roman; and he proved able to make excellent use of this threefold status."[7]

---

2. Sanders, *Paul*, 11.

3. See Galatians 1:14.

4. While Acts 22:3 suggests he studies under Gamaliel in Jerusalem, Paul contradicts this assertion by suggesting he has not been to Jerusalem yet. See Galatians 1:22.

5. See Acts 26:24; 1 Corinthians 15:32–33.

6. Ries and Ries, *The Origin of Brands*, 98.

7. Grant, *Saint Paul*, 15.

After his conversion Paul spent his career journeying throughout the known world. His first mentor, Barnabas, took him to Antioch, one of the first mixed Jewish/Gentile churches. It was during this extended stay that Paul understood the unique challenges facing the church.

THE POWER OF PRUNING THE MESSAGE AND AUDIENCE

Paul's letters tend to address issues and problems in the local church. Retired Princeton professor John Gager writes that Paul was engaging in "damage control."[8] The apostle's writings provide insight into some of the challenges facing the early church. His letters only clarify theology, they do not create systematic theology. Most of his writings are related to behavior, rather than doctrine. Some of his pastoral letters are considered "advice" to his colleagues (i.e., Timothy and Titus), giving them counsel "in their supervision of churches."[9]

By keeping in touch with all of his churches, Paul uniquely influenced their theology. Had he left each of his missionary endeavors without follow-up, the church may have taken a different shape. However, he employed a powerful branding strategy called *pruning*.

Corporate pruning is similar to garden pruning. It is used when companies grow too quickly by diversifying in areas where they may not have expertise. Sears, originally a hardware store, gradually morphed into a store offering everything from lawn mowers to eyeglasses, car repair to portrait studio services, and much more. The strategy worked at first, but after years of decline, the company began the arduous task of cutting back peripheral products and services in order to focus on some key areas and rebuild customer loyalty. Such pruning builds strength and stability.[10]

Paul's ability to prune is evident in his letters, which can be described as a typical pastor's follow-up remarks to his congregation. His letters were often written to clarify or address concerns that arose from living out the new Christian faith, such as dietary rules, circumcision, how Christianity related to Judaism, etc.

8. Gager, *Reinventing Paul*, 77.

9. Grant, *Saint Paul*, 4.

10. Ries and Ries, *The Origin of Brands*, 206. See Malcolm Gladwell's discussion on McDonald's Corporation in *Blink*.

Paul's message was very simple, but urgent. He believed that the eschatological countdown had begun.[11] He focused on Christ—the Son sent from God, crucified for the sake of humanity, and raised from the dead—who would soon return for those who believed in him so they would be with him forever. This was Paul's central message. "Paul's gospel, like that of others, also included admonition to live by the highest ethical and moral standard: 'May your spirit and soul and body be kept sound and blameless at the coming of our Lord Jesus Christ' (1 Thessalonians 5:23)."[12]

DOMINANT SELLING IDEA

Brand building is divided into two phases. The first involves crafting the primary message or the dominant selling idea. The second is executing the elements needed to maintain a lasting brand.[13] Once the dominant selling idea is solidified, a marketing strategy that defines how the message will be communicated can be developed.

In circa 45, Paul and Barnabas set out on their first missionary journey to Syria, Cyprus, and Asia Minor, a trip that lasted several years. During that time, they experienced rebuke and rejection from the Jews of the Dispersion, who were unable to accept the message of Jesus as the Messiah. "At the first two Roman colonies [Paul] is recorded to have visited Psidian Antioch (Yalvac) and Lystra (Hatunsaray)—both in central Asia Minor—where he attracted the unfavorable attention of the colonial authorities. They expelled him and his companion Barnabas from the first of these towns, after the Jews agitated for such action. The two missionaries were also forcibly ejected from Lystra, though this was probably the act of a Jewish mob rather than of the colonial administration."[14]

Paul's primary audience slowly evolved with his message. While Peter directed most of his efforts at reaching Jerusalem Jews, Paul eventually directed his focus on the Gentiles of his own Dispersion. His central message began taking shape and becoming more specific: he believed the same salvation offered to the Jews was now an open invitation to the rest

---

11. Wenham, *Paul*, 53.
12. Sanders, *Paul*, 27.
13. Schley and Nichols, *Why Johnny Can't Brand*, 51.
14. Grant, *Saint Paul*, 179.

of the world. This was Paul's dominant selling idea. Consequently, questions concerning non-Jews and their allegiance to Jewish culture and practice began surfacing and became a contentious issue in Jerusalem.

Paul took his second missionary journey through a large portion of Asia Minor, including Macedonia and Achaea. This three-year voyage opened up opportunities for him to have numerous conversations with non-Gentiles, including Gallio, the Roman governor of Achaea. It was during his second and third missionary trips that his target audience shifted dramatically. By that point, Paul viewed himself as an apostle to the Gentiles, "I will not venture to speak of anything except what Christ has accomplished through me in leading the Gentiles to obey God by what I have said and done."[15]

EVERY BRAND NEEDS AN ENEMY

One of the well-known strategies for establishing a brand is to create an enemy—a counter position or a competitor. "Every new [brand] category enters a mind by positioning itself against an existing category."[16] By treating an existing category as its enemy, the consumer is forced to make a decision based on loyalty. If a brand can position itself as superior it will gain the confidence of the consumer.

The competition is key to the brand's development and sustainability. Coca-Cola and Pepsi-Cola's ruthless competitiveness is legendary. Both companies spend hundreds of millions of dollars every year to establish the other as the enemy. Over the last twenty years, while Pepsi-Cola has outscored Coke in taste tests, Coca-Cola has outsold Pepsi consistently. Best-selling author Malcolm Gladwell suggests, "we transfer our sensation of the Coca-Cola taste all of the unconscious associations we have of the brand, the image, the can, and even the unmistakable red of the logo."[17]

Paul's competition was with the Jerusalem Jews. Upon arriving in Jerusalem in circa 58 (his third visit recorded in the letters, and fifth according to Acts), he was accosted and detained by the Roman authorities in order to save his life from angry Jews. Paul's disagreements with the Jerusalem Jews is widely noted because of his personal belief in accepting

---

15. Romans 15:18.

16. Ries and Ries, *The Origin of Brands*, 259.

17. Gladwell, *Blink*, 156–159. See also Lindstrom, *Brand Sense*, 191.

non-Jews into the community, and giving them a pass on Jewish practices such as circumcision, food restrictions, and idol worship.[18] Faithful Jews deemed some of Paul's views as offensive and unacceptable.

Paul's discontentment with the Jerusalem Jews (led by Peter), created a sense of rivalry. This feeling of animosity and disagreement may have given Paul the sympathy vote.[19]

HOW PAUL COMMUNICATED HIS MESSAGE

The apostle had a demanding task in communicating his message to a diverse audience that spanned from Jerusalem to Asia Minor. While Paul's message was fairly simple—proclaiming the crucified and resurrected Savior—his strategy was as diverse as his audience. In many respects he operated under the motto "any means necessary" to make an impact. His multicultural and linguistic ability became an asset as he attempted to reach his audience.

Paul branded his message through personal presentations, debates, and letter writing campaigns. His new ideas were part of his marketing strategy to get attention. Branding The apostle Paul would stay in urban cities where his efforts were filled with strategic endeavors to organize small congregations. He would start by preaching in local synagogues. There are numerous sources to suggest it was not uncommon for Gentiles to attend synagogues throughout the Greco-Roman world. This was an advantage, assuming the Gentiles already had some biblical knowledge regarding his message.[20]

Paul's personal conversion story was compelling. It was hard to believe, yet seemed authentic. His former life—a self-described Christian-hating Pharisee turned evangelizing Jewish apostle—helped shape his persona into a sympathetic, loving teacher. His dramatic conversion—being blinded at the feet of Jesus Christ, his stories of being shipwrecked,

---

18. While many of Paul's assertions on dietary laws and circumcision may seem trivial to us now, it was his changing theological belief that Jews were no longer the "chosen" group of God that raised concerns among his colleagues. Paul asserts in Romans that *both* Jews and Gentiles have freedom through salvation. Moreover, the salvation plan has been flipped, and Gentiles will enter first as the people of God. See Romans 9–11 for reference.

19. I am not suggesting that Paul deliberately created animosity among the Jewish leaders in order to advance his message. See Acts 15–16 for a full account of the Jerusalem council.

20. Gager, *Reinventing Paul*, 51.

flogged, beaten, robbed, living like a middle-class wage earner, working with his hands making tents—created a mystique that seemed all too attractive. Godin says, "Either you're going to tell stories that spread, or you will become irrelevant."[21] Paul's ability to tell stories was a key contributor in branding his message.

At least thirteen books of the New Testament are credited to Paul. Through letters, homilies, rhetoric, pastoral epistles, and theological narratives he slowly branded his message, which he delivered through sermons, explanations, guidance, condemnation, clarification, and advice. His letters served as a personal substitute while he was traveling to other port cities or was detained.[22]

PAUL'S USE OF RHETORIC

The persuasive delivery used by the apostle was a common technique of the time. This skill would have been an important part of the educational curriculum used in the Greco-Roman world. Furthermore, it may have served as a mark of high accomplishment for a Diasporic Jew living in or outside of Jerusalem.[23]

There are three types of rhetoric, adapted by Aristotle, that are applied to New Testament literature: judicial or forensic rhetoric was commonly used in the court of law; deliberative rhetoric was used in an assembly; and epideictic rhetoric was used in a funeral oration, or in a speech given to laud a particular person. While Paul was able to use all three styles, he favored deliberative rhetoric. Bible scholar Ben Witherington III describes how Paul used this style:

> Over the course of time, speakers learned more and less effective ways of arranging a speech. The standard forms from the time of Aristotle through the time of Paul and beyond entailed the following: The speaker would attend to his own ethos or character, with an attempt to make the audience favorably disposed toward himself and so his topic. Then the rhetor would focus on logos, the actual acts of persuasion, through argumentation and insinuation. Finally, the speech would turn to pathos, the emotional appeal meant to arouse the deeper passions and so move the audience to convict or exonerate, act or refrain from action, applaud or boo.[24]

21. Godin, *All Marketers Are Liars*, 1.
22. Galambush, *The Reluctant Parting*, 117.
23. See Bonner, *Education in Ancient Rome*, 64.
24. Witherington, *The Paul Quest*, 117.

DEVELOPING AND TRANSMITTING THE MESSAGE

Paul's greatest challenge was communicating in absentia to a mostly illiterate audience. At best, only 10 to 20 percent of the Greco-Roman world may have been literate.[25] His letters were intended to be read aloud by a colleague who knew him well, who in turn could elaborate or explain portions of the letter that may have been unclear.

It is interesting to note the apostle's letters were extremely lengthy in comparison to other letters of the day. His letters are considered to be long-winded and hard to understand, even in comparison to Cicero (a first-century writer).[26] Because of the time and expense involved in letter writing, most letters were short and direct. Paul's letters are an exception, in particular, among religious writings.

The development of Paul's messages relied heavily upon a network of co-writers, secretaries, and fellow sojourners. Four of his letters are credited to both "Paul and Timothy" (2 Corinthians, Philippians, Colossians, and Philemon) and two from "Paul, Silvanus, and Timothy" (1 and 2 Thessalonians) even though the primary and secondary writers are not given.

In addition, much labor of writing was left to *amanuenses*, or scribes who were given a wide degree of independence in their writing. "That is, the secretary had to be skilled enough to know the personality, and if possible, the writing style, of the author, but also to know what would be communicated well with a particular audience."[27] Because each of his letters was unique to the contextual and cultural setting, he would tailor the letter sections again and again to suit his purpose and audience.[28]

Some of the Paul's letters are thought to be written by other sources, and may not have been endorsed by the apostle. Six disputed letters (2 Thessalonians, Ephesians, Colossians, 1 and 2 Timothy, and Titus) are attributed to pseudonymity, the act of writing under a well-known figure's name. This practice was widely used in both Jewish and Hellenistic circles.[29]

---

25. Ibid., 92.

26. See 2 Peter 3:16; 2 Corinthians 10:10.

27. Witherington, *The Paul Quest*, 100. See also Raymond Collins, *Introduction to the New Testament*.

28. Witherington, *The Paul Quest*, 100, 105.

29. Galambush, *The Reluctant Parting*, 119.

Paul's messages were largely written to people living in urban centers. His strategy to reach a wider audience can be seen through his letter writing campaigns and missionary trips to places such as Ephesus, Philippi, Corinth, Antioch, and Psidian, where his Judaism and his Roman citizenship would enable him to thrive. "Paul knew that the cities and Roman roads that linked them were keys to reaching the Mediterranean Crescent quickly for Christ."[30]

PAUL'S THEOLOGICAL APPROACH

Paul's primary objective was to convert Gentiles.[31] His approach and theology was often misunderstood or misaligned with the church in Jerusalem and Jewish Christians. Retired Claremont professor Burton Mack suggests, "Christianity was born of a [Jewish] law-gospel conflict."[32] Paul believed many of the Jewish customs and traditions were not relevant to Gentile believers. Additionally, he believed Gentiles were to be viewed as equal sojourners with Jews.

Scholars have regularly questioned Paul's commitment to Judaism. How could he be a faithful Jew, who believed in the covenantal laws governing Israel's salvation? Scholar E.P. Sanders has vigorously argued for a new view of Judaism by coining the term, *covenantal nomism* to describe the ancient law of Judaism and redemption:

> ". . . one's place in God's plan is established on the basis of the covenant and that the covenant requires . . . obedience to its commandments, while providing means of atonement for transgression."[33]

Sanders suggests that the covenant to Israel is "offered, established, and maintained by God; the law is Israel's part of the bargain."[34] Therefore Paul was working under two tracks, a Jewish understanding of salvation and a Gentile one.[35] His theological and practical understanding can be summed up in 1 Corinthians 9:19–23:

30. Witherington *The Paul Quest,* 115.

31. See Romans 11:13, 15:16; Galatians 2:2, 1:16, 2:7–9.

32. Mack, *Who Wrote the New Testament,* 106.

33. Sanders, *Paul and Palestinian Judaism,* 75.

34. Gager, *Reinventing Paul,* 46.

35. See Romans concerning Paul's view of the necessity of keeping the law. Many writers misread this section as a universal endorsement of negating the law, rather than bearing in mind who Paul's audience was.

Though I am free and belong to no man, I make myself a slave to everyone, to win as many as possible. [20]To the Jews I became like a Jew, to win the Jews. To those under the law I became like one under the law (though I myself am not under the law), so as to win those under the law. [21]To those not having the law I became like one not having the law (though I am not free from God's law but am under Christ's law), so as to win those not having the law. [22]To the weak I became weak, to win the weak. I have become all things to all men so that by all possible means I might save some. [23]I do all this for the sake of the gospel, that I may share in its blessings.

His missionary approach therefore was contextual.[36] It gave him the freedom to live as a Jew (food, practice, circumcision, festivals, etc.) to reach Jews. In the same way, in order to reach Gentiles, he would live as *they* did (food, idolatry, and teaching of non-circumcision). Paul's slogan to the Gentiles may have been "freedom from the law," meaning they could become Christians and join the house of Israel without keeping certain aspects of the Jewish law.[37]

Paul carefully crafted a unifying brand. The message of exclusivity in God's favor, which existed in Jewish culture, was replaced by a message of inclusion directed to the Gentiles. Paul's branding can be identified throughout his writings. He repeated his idea of inclusivity throughout his many correspondences, which also revealed his understanding of the truth that brand messaging must be repeated multiple times and in numerous ways. "Repetition has been one of the most prominent techniques used by advertisers to ensure a message is understood and remembered by the consumer."[38] The vision must be communicated repeatedly so that it connects. Paul's unifying message can be seen in the following example:

ROMANS 10:12

For there is no difference between Jew and Gentile—the same Lord is Lord of all and richly blesses all who call on him . . .

---

36. This may be why Paul didn't quote the bible to the Athenians in Acts 17. He knew how to reach them in their culture by quoting their poets, not his prophets. See McLaren, *Church on the Other Side*, 78.

37. Gager, *Reinventing Paul*, 105.

38. Lindstrom, *Brand Sense*, 16.

1 Corinthians 12:13

For we were all baptized by one Spirit into one body—whether Jews or Greeks, slave or free—and we were all given the one Spirit to drink.

Galatians 3:28

There is neither Jew nor Greek, slave nor free, male nor female, for you are all one in Christ Jesus.

Colossians 3:11

Here there is no Greek or Jew, circumcised or uncircumcised, barbarian, Scythian, slave or free, but Christ is all, and is in all.[/TABLE]

ADAPTING TO THE TARGET AUDIENCE

Every brand manager must know his prospective audience. What is their culture? How do they communicate best? What are the major issues they face? How do they make decisions? Once this data is collected, the manager can then address the greatest need.

The conflict between the church fathers in Jerusalem is widely understood through the records of Acts. However, it does seem that Paul entered some kind of compromise on occasion. While he vehemently defended Titus, a Greek, from being circumcised,[39] he encouraged Timothy to be circumcised for the sake of the gospel.[40]

This kind of compromise could be misconstrued as the apostle changing his mind. However, it should be noted his advice normally sided with his audience's social context.

Paul had the uncanny ability to understand the social implications facing each of the communities he addressed. His letters were written to address and resolve specific problems or to serve as progress notes—follow-up letters to encourage and offer advice. In his letter to the Galatians, for example, he did not use his usual letter outline, instead, he omitted an opening thanksgiving, greetings to particular people, wishes for good health, and talk of his present or future travels. His rhetoric was stoic and direct and appears to outline a well-defined argument.

His use of rhetoric demonstrated his personal concern for his audience. He employed strategies that would work effectively on his mainly

---

39. Galatians 2:3.
40. Acts 16:2–3.

Gentile audience. "He wanted his proclamation and persuasion to be a word on target."[41] Paul used skillful arguments to convey his message while being careful not to breach his commitment to the truth.

Paul was worried about the Galatians, who faced increased pressure by some Judaizers to succumb to Jewish laws and traditions. He believed if they gave way to the pressure, they would easily lose sight of salvation by faith in Christ. Paul's key verse, "It is for freedom that Christ has set us free. Stand firm, then, and do not let yourselves be burdened again by a yoke of slavery" (Galatians 5:1), demonstrated his deep desire for the young church to stand firm and not lose sight of God's accepting grace.

In the same spirit, Paul wrote to the other churches addressing their unique situations. Just as he compelled the church in Galatians not to conform, he wrote to the church of Philippi to be unified and in harmony. By way of acknowledging a gift sent to him by the church with Epaphroditus,[42] the apostle wrote a letter of thanks, and in addition compelled the church to live with joy in their hearts. Paul's invitation to stop complaining and live in harmony evoked a sense of teamwork among the church.[43] He thought the Galatians might be adhering to the law too closely ["the only thing that counts is faith expressing itself in love" (5:6)], and believed the church of Corinth was not keeping the law enough, "keeping God's commands is what counts" (1 Corinthians 7:19).

His letter to the Corinthians took on an entirely different tone from his other letters. He was concerned with the young Christian community he established during his second missionary journey. These early Christians faced harmful influences around them in a corrupt city filled with sinful living.

The young Corinthian church was confused. Some were mixing their pagan traditions with Christian teachings, which included deviant opinions about sexual practices. At the same time, there were others who took the opposite extreme and had written the apostle asking if it was better for "a man not to touch a woman."[44]

41. Witherington, *The Paul Quest*, 126.

42. Galatians 4:18.

43. The apostle uses the metaphor of a race or team to encourage continuity in the Christian life. See Philippians 3:13,14; 1 Corinthians 9:24–27; 1 Timothy 4:7–10; 2 Timothy 4:7,8.

44. See 1 Corinthians 7:1. Also see Ehrman, *Peter, Paul, and Mary Magdalene*, 147–78.

His firsthand knowledge of the Corinthian community gave him the authority to address its current situation. Paul's letters were framed to encourage the church members to live Godly lives, regardless of the sexual problems facing the church (6:9–20), the immorality of some of the members, or the lawsuits cropping up between some Christians (5:1–6:8). He urged the Corinthian church to live in unity: "I appeal to you, brothers, in the name of Jesus Christ, that all of you agree with one another so that there may be no divisions among you and that you may be perfectly united in mind and thought" (1:10). He tailored his message based on the audience he was addressing.

URGENCY AND IMMEDIACY IN THE MESSAGE

The success of a brand is dependent on action. The purpose of creating brand identity is to persuade the consumer or audience to act upon the message. Paul created a sense of urgency by using the language of prediction throughout his apocalyptic writing.[45] His eschatological perspective was the driving force behind his zeal.

Paul believed that Christ's return was imminent.[46] This sentiment was the catalyst for intense evangelism. He used the term *apocalypse* to refer to final future events.[47] Paul certified that his revelations came from Jesus Christ himself (Galatians 1:12). This sense of urgency was the sole motivator for Paul's messages. Many of his responses to personal issues are better understood in light of the eschatological dynamic that exists. For example, his response to the Corinthians on why it would be better to stay unmarried: "I am saying this for your own good, not to restrict you, but that you may live in a right way in undivided devotion to the Lord,"[48] sheds light on his thinking, since the "world in its present form is passing away."[49]

The apostle's earliest book, Thessalonians, provides a helpful look at the apocalyptic nature that drove the early church. Paul praised the church for its faithful living, and for treating its members with love (4:3–8).

---

45. 1 Thessalonians 4:13; 5–11; 1 Corinthians 7:29–31; Romans 13:11–14.

46. 1 Corinthians 15:12–19; 1 Thessalonians 4:2–6,15; 2 Thessalonians 3:6,10,12; Galatians 5:21.

47. 1 Corinthians 1:7; Romans 8:19.

48. 1 Corinthians 7:35.

49. 1 Corinthians 7:29–31.

The church was isolated by the pagan society that was persecuting them. Despite Paul's message of the imminent apocalypse, he wrote words of reassurance and peace (1 Thessalonians 2:14–16) to the persecuted. Many in the church were also confused about an afterlife. Such concern for the dead was a familiar theme in the Eastern Mediterranean world. Burial traditions and taboo spiritual practices were rampant. Paul clarified his theology on death, and reminded the Thessalonians of the reward that awaited them upon Christ's return (4:13–18).

Jewish apocalyptic thoughts were clearly communicated through his letter to the Thessalonians. His use of vivid imagery, "from the wrath that is coming" (1:10) and the promise that "God has destined us not for wrath but for . . . salvation" (5:9) illustrates the apocalyptic sentiment that existed in the early church.[50] The Thessalonian letter also demonstrated how "originally Jewish apocalyptic ideas could be transmitted to a Gentile Christian community."[51] Paul helped them see the reward that was theirs, if they remained faithful.

How did this obscure first century figure become the leader of the Christian church? Paul is never mentioned in the synoptic gospels. Furthermore, he rarely quotes Jesus' teachings or life. Paul overcame monumental spiritual obstacles, such as being a Christian killer and prominent Pharisee. He became a co-leader with the original disciples and was primarily responsible for advancing the Jesus message throughout the known world.

What gave Paul the edge? How did he succeed in developing a brand that catapulted Christianity into one of the most powerful world religions? Paul's secret weapon is perhaps what modern companies and brand experts consider to be the single most valuable element: authenticity.

THE APPEAL AND RISK OF AUTHENTICITY

As stated earlier, every company must have a story. Furthermore, the story must be compelling, sentimental, and appear authentic. If there is no story, the company will fabricate one. The story of Juan Valdez, the Columbian farmer, established "100% Colombian coffee" as a global brand. The fictionalized farmer (a paid New York actor) was hired by

50. Mack, *Who Wrote the New Testament*, 109–11.

51. Segal, *Paul the Convert*, 165.

the National Federation of Coffee Growers of Colombia. Jim Hardison, creative director the of character, and brand consultant for the firm said, "Juan Valdez taps into a fundamental human truth, that the things we savor the most are the hardest earned."[52] The public connected emotionally to the character as an authentic, hardworking person.

Paul's transformation and his related testimony is riveting. His story, letters, and life were all authentic.[53] His story was believable, and his actions supported his story. Moreover, his willingness to suffer for his message deepened the sense of his authenticity.

Paul's letters demonstrated a personal touch, a spirit of one who cared deeply about his audience. He wrote to the Romans before he even met them in person, commending them for their faith, which was being reported around the world (v. 8), and sharing his desire to see them soon (v.11). He also wrote his manifesto for them in painstaking detail, elaborating on the plan of salvation for both Jews and Gentiles (v. 14).

Paul wrote his letters with the familiarity of a well-loved brother. His letters reveal the personal affection of someone who lived with and toiled alongside the early Christian community: "I always thank God for you . . . " (1 Corinthians 1:4); he quickly and concisely addressed the pressing issue facing the Galatians, "I am astonished that you are so quickly deserting the one who called you by the grace of Christ and are turning to a different gospel" (Galatians 1:6).

The most revealing and personal side of his letters is found in the closing remarks of Colossians, where Paul expressed his deeply personal wishes and greetings to the church. He sent greetings from fellow sojourners Epaphras, Mark, Barnabas, Luke, and Demas, and he gave greetings to brothers at Laodicea, and to Nympha and the church in her house (Colossians 4:10–16). His personal connection with these communities and his frequent follow-up letters developed an authentic relationship between the apostle and the new Christian churches that he helped establish.

Paul's ability to take a strange religious sect and shape it into one of the most powerful religions in the world is worth noting. His ability to develop his message through careful strategic steps exemplifies the power of modern branding.

52. Breen, "Who Do You Love?" *Fast Company*, Issue 115.

53. The word "authentic" is derived from the Greek *authentikos,* meaning "original."

PART TWO

6

Confronting the Enemy

Addressing the Critical Issues Facing Your Church

If you know the enemy and know yourself
you need not fear the results of a hundred battles.

—SUN TZU

THE GREAT STEAK DEBATE

THE CITY OF PHILADELPHIA is famous for its Philly cheesesteak. Philadelphians are proud of the fact that the cheesesteak was invented in their historic town. The question of *who* has the best cheesesteak has fostered a warlike rivalry between two cheesesteak joints: Pat's and Geno's.

The buzz generated by these two cheesesteak joints has risen to monumental proportions. For example, if you were to take a cab to Geno's, you would find it in the heart of South Philadelphia, randomly situated between row homes and industrial businesses. Geno's is open twenty-four hours a day—with people lined up around the small diner waiting to order one thing: the cheesesteak. It isn't uncommon to see limousines parked along the narrow street, with celebrities or city leaders waiting in line along the sidewalk for their turn to order the world famous cheesesteak.

Alongside the small shack where Geno's men work over the hot grills are hundreds of framed pictures of every imaginable celebrity who has made the pilgrimage to this famous destination. Remember, there is no VIP treatment at Geno's. *Everybody* stands in line for the steak sandwich. If you want to taste the famous cheese fries and get a drink with your meal, you must stand in another line! If you want to add condiments, you must get your own—self-serve along the street. There are only a handful of picnic tables outside the joint, so most people eat while standing, trying not to drip the greasy sauce on their clothing. Despite the few amenities, the environment surrounding Geno's maintains a clean feel. How did Geno's become so famous? According to the story (remember all brands have a meta-narrative) Geno's dad started the business in 1966 with $6.00 in his hand, two boxes of steaks, and some hotdogs.[1] From there the business exploded. Every successful brand must also have an enemy. In Geno's case, it is Pat's Cheesesteak, right across the street! If you are standing in line at Geno's, all you have to do is turn 180 degrees to view another long line of people waiting to try Pat's Cheesesteak. Both joints are located on Passyunk Avenue near Ninth Street in the heart of South Philly. The environment surrounding Pat's joint is very similar to Geno's: bare and simple. Pat's also offers only a few picnic tables, and condiments alongside the road. However there are some differences.

If Geno's joint is clean and shiny, Pat's is the opposite. It reflects the run-down part of the city—raw and urban. There are no pictures of celebrities around Pat's building. However the line is just as long as Geno's. Emblazoned in front of Pat's humble building is a historical sign announcing that this was the place where the original philly cheesesteak was created. The story of Pat's King of Steak begins in the 1930s. Pat had a modest hotdog stand at the base of the famous Italian Market in South Philadelphia. One day he decided to make himself something different for lunch, so he sent for some chopped meat from the butcher shop. He cooked the meat on his hotdog grill, placed it into an Italian roll, and dressed it with some onions. He was just about to take a bite when a cab driver who ate a hotdog from Pat's every day asked what he had there. Pat said that it was his lunch. The cabbie insisted that Pat make him one. The cabbie took one bite and said to Pat, "Hey . . . forget 'bout those hotdogs, you should sell these." The steak sandwich was born.[2]

---

1. See www.patskingofsteaks.com for the full story.
2. Ibid.

The competition between Pat's and Geno's is part of the meta-narrative of Philadelphia. There are countless articles, blogs, and news reports commenting on which joint offers the better steak sandwich.

TOURIST TRAP

The recipe for the cheesesteak includes basic ingredients: thin pieces of steak, fried onions, and cheesewhiz drenched on a long roll. If you were to compare these sandwiches to other cheesesteaks offered around the city of Philadelphia, you might discover better sandwiches. So what entices hundreds of thousands of city dwellers and tourists to make the trek into South Philly to Pat's or Geno's? *Their story.*

Every brand must have an enemy. Have you noticed most gas stations are clustered together at the same intersection? They will either be right next to each other or across from one another. Their success is dependent on their competition. Consider the following brands that are successful in competing with one another:

Coke v. Pepsi
Burger King v. McDonald's
Starbucks v. Dunkin' Donuts
Walmart v. Target
Borders v. Barnes and Nobles
Apple v. Microsoft
Volvo v. BMW
Costco v. Sams
Adidas v. Puma

DEFINING YOUR COMPETITION

Remember, every brand has an enemy. The enemy may be contrived in order to build one's reputation. Al and Laura Ries say, "Every new [brand] category enters a mind by positioning itself against an existing category."[3] What are the critical issues competing against your church? What is preventing people from attending? While the church may not have contrived enemies, it certainly has its share of competitors. What is taking your constituency (clients, customers, volunteers, etc.) away from your organization?

3. Ries and Ries, *The Origin of Brands*, 259.

Every week churches compete against something that keeps their members and potential visitors from attending services. Some basic examples may be the local little league games or Sunday sports on television. David Murrow suggests in his book *Why Men Hate Going to Church*, "Sports, career, hobbies, outdoor recreation, wealth building, and even video games reflect men's core values. Competitive environments allow men to reach for greatness. Church does not."[4] According to Murrow, churches are designed more for women than men.

If you can identify the issues (what I call enemies) that are preventing your potential attendees from engaging in church, you can then begin to make changes that may attract your target audience. Some of the enemies that churches face may be localized, such as sports and recreation. However, there are also philosophical enemies that impact ecclesiology and theology. In this chapter, I will address some of the larger issues facing the church.

In his monograph to the best-selling *Good to Great*, Jim Collins suggests we must determine the resources given to the organization in order to decide what can be leveraged. In *Good to Great*, he says that companies must define their "hedgehog concept." However, within the social sector the financial bottom line is not the end result, therefore the economic engine must be reevaluated. According to Collins, the economic engine consists of three basic components: time, money, and brand.[5] If an organization such as a church can identify the challenges impeding productivity and address them, it may be able to turn these liabilities into collateral.

My wife and I moved to New Hope Church in Burtonsville, Maryland in 2003. After living in Southern California for three years, we were looking forward to moving back home, especially with a baby on the way. New Hope is a unique congregation; it is one of the only Adventist churches (among fifty-eight in the Washington/Baltimore corridor) that have a progressive worship service.

The service attracts many visitors each week, many of whom had been burned by organized religion at some point. Within four years, church attendance increased 144 percent, and financial donations nearly doubled. In 2004, New Hope experienced more baptisms than any other year in the history of the church. According to the measuring tools used

4. Murrow, *Why Men Hate Going to Church*, 17.

5. Collins, *Good to Great*, 18.

by Natural Church Development, New Hope is one of the healthiest congregations in the United States. In addition, it falls in the top 5 percent of U.S. congregations for being multiracial and multicultural.

Despite the positive growth, however, there are some critical issues facing the future health and stability of New Hope—or any Christian church. While the church is growing numerically, is its health substantive? Are the members exhibiting spiritual growth and discipleship? Is the church living out authentic Christian values, or has the congregation fallen prey to the American values of consumerism and relativism? Albert Y. Hsu writes, "Consumer culture is a self-perpetuating phenomenon. The abundance of goods creates a class of consumers who work to afford to consume, which generates more demand for more goods, which creates more consumers. And it goes on."[6] The critical issues facing New Hope Church are similar to those facing many American churches. It is important to identify the issues first, in order to understand and address them. If you understand these conflicting issues as your enemy or competition, you can be better prepared to develop a plan that addresses them contextually.

THE PROPHETIC CALLING

The leadership challenge in pastoral ministry requires a prophetic calling. The role of the pastor is to examine the spiritual health of his or her congregation, chart a course, proclaim the vision, and move the community to a better place. This is how you develop a consistent brand.

The prophets in the Old Testament always proclaimed a unique message that required the people to change. The prophets offered an alternative truth. They never claimed that the Israelites were living in a perfect era in their history. It was the role of the prophets to hold up a mirror to reflect the real state in which the people were living. Likewise, a church leader must have the prophetic insight to understand the state of his or her congregation, to highlight the path for transformation, and diligently lead his or her community toward its goal through the power and influence of the Holy Spirit.

Effective marketers keep a careful eye on continually changing trends in order to reach out to the consumer with their product. The product rarely changes, however, the method of reaching the audience

6. Hsu, *The Suburban Christian*, 82.

always does.[7] In fact, many companies take pride in the authenticity of their product. For instance, Kentucky Fried Chicken claims to keep the General's eleven herbs and spices locked in vault; Coke and Pepsi will not divulge their secret formula.

In the 1980s, Coke attempted brand suicide when it tried to change its recipe by creating New Coke. The church doesn't have to change its recipe because it [the message] is already life transforming. It must, however, address the critical issues that are shaping the way it sells its product, the gospel.

In the midst of our increased attendance and financial abundance, New Hope has identified several critical issues that could destroy our momentum. As you read through the issues that threaten to compromise New Hope's growth, consider the context of some of the challenges facing your congregation.

There are four critical factors threatening New Hope's vitality. First, the growing multiethnic presence in the church could wane due to the monoculture of the surrounding communities in our county. Second, as our church members and the neighboring community become wealthier, the influences of consumerism and materialism threaten to diminish our awareness of the needs of others, both at home and abroad. The quest for personal fortune may prevent Christians from responding charitably in authentic ways. Third, communication through nontraditional media is shifting as the church attracts a younger audience. The fourth and final critical issue New Hope faces is the postmodern influence that is pervasive within the greater culture. If the church doesn't identify the trends that accompany postmodern culture, we will not be able to reach out in loving and effective ways. Like many churches in America that are deeply rooted in Protestant, Newtonian linear thinking, New Hope is faced with a challenge: can we change our strategy and implementation to reach the wider, secular community?

---

7. While most people believe that the message never changes, only the means of communicating it, I believe that the message is never left untouched. Influenced heavily by Shane Hipps, I believe that even the message, such as the gospel, is often altered when we contextually convey the meta-narrative. See Hipps, *The Hidden Power,* 30.

7

Addressing the Multicultural Clash

I was the son of an immigrant. I experienced bigotry, intolerance, and prejudice, even as so many of you have. Instead of allowing these things to embitter me, I took them as spurs to more strenuous effort.

—ANDRE BERNARD BURUCH

THE RACIAL DIVIDE IN America has created an enormous rift in Christian fellowship. How can we be light bearers of the gospel if we cannot worship and grow together? Racism is widely accepted within our churches; it is one of the most insidious enemies that has crept into the Protestant church. In fact, we, the church, have become so accustomed to this divide that we cannot see the sin that exists in segregated worship. If the brand (identity) of the church is about love and acceptance, how can we reflect this through our worship and lifestyles?

Curtiss Paul DeYoung, professor of reconciliation at Bethel, suggests, "Multiracial congregations will be called on in the years ahead to use their experience to provide a healing salve for the wounds of racial division, cultural misunderstandings, and even the lingering pain of traumatic events."[1]

The challenge for the church is to be a prophetic mouthpiece in the community. This is risky. It means that the church must lead by example, and as such, they will be held up for scrutiny. DeYoung contends, "Multiracial congregations certainly should be centers for community development that address the needs of their neighborhoods and places of refuge for people of color who are experiencing the daily assault of racism."[2]

1. DeYoung, *United by Faith*, 75.
2. Ibid., 141.

New Hope Church has remained a multiracial congregation by intentionally marketing this point. New Hope may be one of the only fully integrated congregations in the country in terms of racial, cultural, and generational diversity. Our commitment to racial and social development positions us to speak on race and equality. Yet we have been able to embrace our differences without calling undue attention to our diversity. At the same time, commonality is found across a range of factors (e.g., preferred style of worship, shared vision for the church, core religious beliefs, etc.) that unite people.

In his book *The Future Is Mestizo*, Virgilio Elizondo challenges the reader to take a stand by supporting those who are marginalized, "In the name of the gospel, cultures have been imposed upon entire nations and different races have been conquered, annihilated, or enslaved as worthless heathens. In the name of defending the law and order of the nations, the church has often stood by silently as the nothings of society have been exploited and deported."[3] Elizondo suggests that churches must work toward racial integration, not assimilation. "Assimilation—to become one and the same—is not the goal. Integration—to be united in our equally respected differences—is the goal."[4]

After residing in the same community for almost a half century, New Hope Church moved from a racially integrated community in Burtonsville, Maryland, to a homogeneous community in Fulton, Maryland, where 80 percent of the neighboring community is White. The test for New Hope now is whether we will be able to preserve our existing eclectic color mix, thereby becoming countercultural. "The present reality of separate White congregations in the United States is rarely justified using the harsh racist rhetoric of the past," Elizondo contends. "In fact, it is rarely considered abnormal or unbiblical to be an all-White congregation. It is a de facto segregation—a product of history or the makeup of one's neighborhood."[5]

One of New Hope's strategies for remaining multicultural is to bridge the gap through worship. Each week our worship and arts presentation attempts to cross over divides of culture, race, and age. New Hope continually strives to find effective ways to create a worship experience that is not "watered down" in order to win everybody. In his essay in

3. Elizondo, *The Future Is Mestizo*, 71.

4. Ibid., 139.

5. Ibid. 123.

Making Room at the Table, Donald Juel suggests that we " . . . presume not only the idea of a community formed from diverse members but the actual formation of such a community through the experience of worship."[6] Although New Hope has not developed a formula, it appears the worship style we are offering is crossing the typical boundaries.

Another strategy has been to hire staff who reflect the diversity we are striving to achieve. David Anderson, author of *Gracism: The Art of Inclusion,* and the senior pastor of Bridgeway Community Church, demonstrates this in his staffing. If you were to visit his congregation in Columbia, Maryland, you would witness the wide range of ethnic diversity not only in his congregation but also in the paid staff.

A number of years ago, I attended a church leadership conference at one of the largest churches in America. The senior pastor's statements of inclusion impressed me. He admitted his church was monocultural, and no longer reflected the changing landscape of the community. On that summer day, he shared his vision with thousands of church leaders; it was time his congregation become open to racial diversity. Five years later, upon attending another leadership conference at the same megachurch, not much had changed. The racial demographics of the congregation were the same, and there were no pastors of color on staff. Hiring staff who represent the diversity of God's family demonstrates to the congregation and the community what you really value.

If your church isn't large enough to hire multiple staff, it is imperative to have people of different ethnic backgrounds serving in leadership positions. My first associate pastoral position was in a three thousand-member congregation. This congregation boasted of its racial diversity. And it was true; the ethnic makeup of the congregation was beautiful. Every hue, language, and culture was represented in the pews. However, upon a closer look, the lay leadership of the congregation was monocultural. Every month during the church board meeting, it was evident where the power lay: within a small segment of Eurocentric members. The lack of diversity within the lay leadership of the congregation prevented a full expression of the church's vision.

6. Juel, *Making Room,* 44.

MULTICULTURAL GROWTH AT NEW HOPE

At my church, New Hope, we have been experiencing phenomenal growth. While the church falls in the top 5 percent of all U.S. congregations for diversity, there are still issues that could threaten the vitality of our congregation.

The church members represent unusual wealth, and could easily become self-absorbed with abundance instead of living out the Christian call to support the needy, many of whom are vulnerable in part because of their racial or ethnic background. Historically, the Christian church has not been a voice for the racially or ethnically marginalized. The multiracial culture may be threatened by the new move into a homogeneous community.

The land surrounding the church has been slowly changing hands from family-owned farms—owned for generations—to land developers who are eager to build multimillion-dollar homes on one-acre parcels. In *United by Faith*, the authors predict a shift that is already taking place in Fulton, Maryland. "The broad population shifts taking place in the United States are expected by the midpoint of the century to produce a country with a racial demographic that is very diverse and without a numeric majority."[7] It is anticipated that Howard County likewise will increasingly become heterogeneous.

While many churches in America are hoping to become multicultural, New Hope is also trying to do so while remaining relevant. Our challenge is not to become more racially diverse, but rather to live out our current rich diversity. But living out our diversity means taking risks. It means that we must be willing for *others* to judge us, disagree with us, and challenge our decisions. We must be willing to make bold decisions in order to do what is right despite potential opposition.

Can New Hope leverage its multicultural makeup as a teaching model for the community? As Howard County evolves and slowly turns "brown," can our church highlight integration and leadership models for embracing and benefiting from that diversity?

The challenge for any pastor or church leader is to respond to the need for change. Most leaders can identify the problem. However, it takes another skill set to address the issues. Many leaders do not want to make waves, or address controversial issues, even when it is right to do

---

7. DeYoung, *United by Faith*, 74.

so. If indeed pastoral ministry requires a prophetic calling, how do we live it? Do we become the catalyst for social change and equality? The Hebrew word for prophet is "nabi." The word "Ro'eh" is a seer, a bit more charismatic than other prophets. Prophets were often seen as visionaries, rebukers of injustice, and social analysts. God generally accepted them as chosen agents, even when they appeared to be insane loners. How can churches like New Hope leverage their influence in the community to be seen as change agents within the spectrum of diversity?

Since New Hope's move to a more homogeneous county, we will need to carefully track our ethnic diversity in the congregation. As the county slowly 'darkens' with first and second-generation immigrants, we believe our congregation can serve as a prophetic voice to the entire community on how to live as a reconciled religious community. The greatest fear for many churches is that by including 'others' into the leadership voice, the congregation will change. I heard one parishioner say, "We will become different, and lose our specialness."

As you look into your congregation, who is missing from your pews? What are the steps you can begin taking to serve as a prophetic voice in your community?

8

God's Bling

Profit v. Prophet

The majority of the world's resources pour into the United States. And as we Americans grow more and more wealthy, money is becoming a kind of narcotic for us. We hardly notice our own prosperity or the poverty of so many others.

—Walter Brueggemann

There are two ways to get enough; one is to continue to accumulate more and more. The other is to desire less.

—G. K. Chesterton

In his classic book *The Prophetic Imagination*, Walter Brueggemann uses the Solomonic achievements as a foundation for the misinterpretation of God's original plan for Israel. Moses' intention was to lead the Israelites out of bondage from Egypt. Their freedom from slavery would release God's people from the disastrous lifestyle they had endured. Unfortunately, they failed to be content with their humble calling. Brueggemann points out that their desire was to replicate the Egyptian dynasty. King Solomon's achievements are a blatant example of the excess and "Canaanization in Israel," or "paganization of Israel."[1] God's people failed to grasp a true understanding of justice and equality. Instead of starting anew, they replicated what they had known in Egypt—reconstructing what they left behind.

---

1. Walter Brueggemann, *The Prophetic Imagination*, 24.

THE BEST THAT MONEY CAN BUY

On January 22, 2005, Donald Trump, 58, and Melania Knauss, 30, were married at the Bethesda by the Sea Church in Palm Beach, Florida.[2] Trump, a self-made billionaire, spared no expense on his third wedding. There were ten thousand flowers, forty-five chefs, a two hundred-pound Grand Marnier cake, and performances by Tony Bennett and Billy Joel. The guest list read like an Emmy Awards roster; it included celebrities such as former President Bill Clinton, Oprah Winfrey, Shaquille O'Neal, and Katie Couric.

Though Trump's wedding may appear outlandish, it does not hold the record for the most expensive wedding in recent history. Lakshmi Mittal, the world's fifth richest man, spent $60 million in honor of his daughter Vanisha's nuptials. The family issued a twenty-page invitation in silver boxes. All of the guests attending the wedding stayed at a five-star Paris hotel for the five-day affair.[3]

The super rich have caught the attention of the ordinary individual. Through modern media and popular television shows, Americans live vicariously through celebrity millionaires and billionaires. Hit television shows such as MTV's *Cribs, The Fabulous Life of . . .,* or *My Super Sweet Sixteen Birthday Party* portray the lavish spending of wealthy individuals.

In a recent episode of MTV's *My Super Sweet Sixteen Birthday Party,* Erica, a young teenager, spent more than $200,000 on her birthday. Her parents hired a famous musician to give a personal concert and also surprised her with a new BMW. As the new car was driven into view, her friends and classmates began screaming with elation. One young man jumped on top of the vehicle and kissed it as if it were a newborn baby. The excessive abundance depicted is similar to numerous other television shows that highlight the outlandish habits of the rich.

It is very easy to observe the spending of the super rich and feel desensitized. The lifestyles projected on the television or magazine covers have created an immunity of sorts—an escapist condition that helps us justify our own relatively excessive spending and consumer-oriented lifestyles—because we do not feel rich in comparison to what we are seeing, and do not think of ourselves as materialists.

2. http://marriage.about.com/od/entrepreneurs/p/donaldtrump.htm.

3. Paul Maidment, "Lakshmi Mittal's $19 Billion Year," *Forbes,* http://www.forbes .com/2005/03/10/cx_pm_0310mittal_bill05.html.

THE REALITY OF THE SUBURBS

There are similarities between the New Hope congregation and the children of Israel. The New Hope community is creating its own "Solomonic achievements." The Washington suburbs provide an easy escape from the reality that exists just a few miles away in the city. Just as the Israelites easily forgot about their humble beginnings as slaves, the New Hope community has become enslaved to the "paganization" of societal temptations. The *Washington Post* noted that residents living in the Washington, D.C., suburbs are among the richest in the country:

> The three most prosperous large counties in the United States are in the Washington suburbs, according to census figures released yesterday, which show that the region has the second-highest income and the least poverty of any major metropolitan area in the country. Rapidly growing Loudoun County has emerged as the wealthiest jurisdiction in the nation, with its households last year having a median income of more than $98,000. It is followed by Fairfax and Howard counties, with Montgomery County not far behind.[4]

While the congregation serves as a powerful witness for racial integration, it also has its challenges. The middle-class American has every opportunity to live a life of abundance without the fear of hunger, loss of education, or health care. "Middle-class North American children face abundance on every hand. Possibilities and opportunities have expanded so greatly that the very shape of life has changed. They can do anything, go anywhere, and be anybody. They see no risk—they can always start over, and they will not starve. The real risk is spiritual. They could lose their souls."[5] How does a pastor encourage a faith community living in that context to do a reality check?

THE CHANGING DEMOGRAPHICS OF THE COMMUNITY

The Fulton community surrounding New Hope has slowly been changing into a metropolitan suburb. The community is nestled in the Baltimore/Washington corridor. The sleepy town of two thousand residents has been known for its large cow pastures, farms, and agricultural development.

4. Goldstein and Keating, "D.C. Suburbs," The *Washington Post*, A–1.
5. Stafford, "Making Do," *Christianity Today*, 60.

But the town is slowly evolving from a rural environment to an urban development, which can result in urban sprawl and ethnic diversity. The city of Fulton is representative of Howard County, where the influx of racial diversity and socio-economic changes have created tensions between the classes and races.

SECOND GENERATION IMMIGRANTS AT NEW HOPE

A growing population of the church consists of second-generation immigrants, who belong to what is known as Generation X.[6] In our church-wide survey, we discovered one-third of the respondents were immigrants. When asked about their citizenship at birth, 62 percent of these reported they are native-born U.S. citizens. This figure suggests they are second-generation immigrants—their parents were born in another country and then immigrated to America.

New Hope has twice as many immigrants as the general population in the Washington metropolitan area. They have chosen not to attend the homogenous, ethnically segregated churches of their parents, and have intentionally determined to raise their children in a multicultural setting. "We realized that our children are growing up in a diverse world. Their neighborhood, school, and friends are diverse, but not their church. That is why we decided to come to New Hope; we wanted our kids to experience diversity in all areas of their lives," said church member Andrea Wells.[7]

The parents of these Xers moved to the United States in search of a better life for their families. This better life consisted of working long, grueling hours—often holding two or three jobs—to achieve the American dream. In a cover story on Generation X in *Time* magazine, a pollster said that idealistic boomer parents left their buster children a difficult legacy: "Divorce. Latchkey kids. Homelessness. Soaring national debt. Bankrupt Social Security. Holes in the ozone layer. Crack. Downsizing and layoffs. Urban deterioration. Gangs. Junk bonds."[8] Xers were often left alone at home, raised by television sets and friends in the neighborhood, while their parents worked away from the home.

6. Also known as Xers or Busters.

7. Comment made during the October, 2007 *Entrance to Membership* class at New Hope Adventist Church.

8. J. Walker Smith as quoted by Margot Hornblower in "Great Expectations," Time, June 9, 1997, 23.

Through their parent's self-sacrifice and unyielding devotion to personal and financial success, second-generation immigrant Xers learned the value of hard work. Even more, they discovered the result of hard work—self-indulgence through wealth. Similar to their parents, many are willing to sacrifice important family time for financial wealth. A close look at the socio-economic status of the people in the pews at New Hope reveals a wealthy congregation. The largest group in the congregation (44 percent) comes from homes where the annual income is $75,000 or higher. Xers were also the generation to grow up without going to church. They have often been labeled as cynical, anti-establishment, and questioners of everything.[9]

A major difference between both generations is their motivation. While immigrant boomers worked out of duty to provide basic needs for their families, the second-generation immigrant Xers are working to fulfill their indulgence, which is influenced by the consumer-driven society that is saturated with materialism. Yet Xers justify *their* extravagant lifestyles and grueling work hours by claiming they are doing it for their kids.

As you brand your church, you must be willing to address the issues that are preventing your congregation from being faithful to its narrative. This will often require theological reflection. For example, if New Hope is going to live out its vision statement, "To be an irresistible influence in the community" the leadership and members will need to address the biblical issues related to wealth, prosperity, and generosity.

What does the Bible say about wealth? What does it say about the poor? What is the responsibility of middle-class Christians, who are among the richest group in the world? Exodus 16 provides a snapshot on wealth, personal belongings, trust, security, and dependence.

> [1]The whole Israelite community set out from Elim and came to the Desert of Sin, which is between Elim and Sinai, on the fifteenth day of the second month after they had come out of Egypt. [2]In the desert the whole community grumbled against Moses and Aaron. [3]The Israelites said to them, "If only we had died by the LORD's hand in Egypt! There we sat around pots of meat and

9. This leads to why postmodern thinking and rationalization is easily accepted and adopted by Xers. I will examine this in greater detail in chapter 10.

ate all the food we wanted, but you have brought us out into this
desert to starve this entire assembly to death."[10]

The children of Israel had been wandering in the desert for approximately two and a half months. They were discouraged, tired, and
starting to have second thoughts about their escape from Egypt. They
had endured severe hardships living in oppressive conditions in Egypt
for four hundred years as slaves. However, after only a few months in
the desert, their painful memories of slavery began to fade and were replaced with skewed memories of grandeur in Egypt. They began wishing
they could return to Egypt because, "There we sat around pots of meat
and ate all the food we wanted . . . "

Scarcity is often demonstrated when we compare ourselves to others or wish we lived in a different place or time. Walter Brueggemann
writes in *Christian Century*:

> "The majority of the world's resources pour into the United
> States. And as we Americans grow more and more wealthy,
> money is becoming a kind of narcotic for us. We hardly notice
> our own prosperity or the poverty of so many others. The great
> contradiction is that we have more and more money and less and
> less generosity—less and less public money for the needy, less
> charity for the neighbor. Consumerism is not simply a marketing
> strategy. It has become a demonic spiritual force among us, and
> the theological question facing us is whether the gospel has the
> power to help us withstand it."[11]

It is easy to feel like we need more than we have, especially when
we are bombarded by images that make us feel like we must have something more. Americans represent only 6 percent of the world's population, however, we consume 40 percent of the world's resources. Ronald
Sider writes, "An abundance of possessions can easily lead us to forget
that God is the source of all goods. Most Christians in the Northern
Hemisphere simply do not believe Jesus' teaching about the deadly dan-
ger of possessions."[12] Jesus warned that it is difficult to be a rich person
and his follower at the same time.[13]

---

10. Exodus 16:1–3.
11. Brueggemann, "The liturgy of abundance," *Christian Century*, 342.
12. Sider, *Rich Christians*, 95.
13. See Matthew 19:23,24; Mark 10:23,25; Luke 6:24.

The use of the word covetousness (it occurs nineteen times in the New Testament) reflects the biblical understanding of the dangers of riches. The Greek word *pleonexia* (translated "covetousness" or "greed") means "striving for material possession."[14] The story of the rich young ruler uses this same term, "Watch out! Be on your guard against all kinds of greed [pleonexia]; a man's life does not consist in the abundance of his possessions."[15]

GOD'S ORIGINAL INTENT ON EQUALITY

God's original intent is a distribution of resources based on equality. There is an interesting theme that runs through Genesis 16. The Israelites had been slaves for four hundred years. These grumbling people were descendents of the original slaves taken into captivity and had known only slavery during their lifetime.

In Egypt, they were all of equal status as low-level slaves. But when God provided the manna, He explained that each person was to take according to his or her *needs*, not his or her *wants*. The principle of want and need is very important, because it runs as a continual theme throughout the Bible. It is not our role to tell God what we want, but rather what we need. And God says he will provide for our needs. Sider writes:

> Rich Christians must be careful not to distort the biblical teaching that God sometimes rewards obedience with material abundance. Wealthy persons who make Christmas baskets and give them to relief agencies have not satisfied God's demand. God wills justice for the poor, not occasional charity. And justice means things like the jubilee and the sabbatical remission of productive resources needed to earn a decent living.[16]

The theme of equality among the rich and poor in the Bible is evident. Sider states that God's design is not for people to live in poverty, hunger, and destitution. There is a deep interest in equality and justice that is carefully woven throughout scripture. In Leviticus 25:10–24, the year of Jubilee demanded for land to be returned every fifty years. In Deuteronomy 15 there is a call for all debts to be forgiven every seven years.

14. Sider, *Rich Christians*, 97.
15. Luke 12:15.
16. Sider, *Rich Christians*, 103.

Every fifty years, God said, the land was to be returned to its original owners. Physical handicaps, death of a breadwinner, or lack of natural ability might cause some families to become poorer than others. But God did not want such disadvantages to lead to ever-increasing extremes of wealth and poverty, with the result that the poor eventually lacked the basic resources to earn a decent livelihood.[17]

Deuteronomy 15:1–15 calls for the cancellation of debts, release of Hebrew slaves, and liberation of soil to take place every seven years. It is interesting to note that Yahweh warns against denying a loan to somebody who is poor in the sixth year, because he or she may not be able to fulfill his or her obligation and may be released in the seventh year:

> [9]Be careful not to harbor this wicked thought: "The seventh year, the year for canceling debts, is near," so that you do not show ill will toward your needy brother and give him nothing. He may then appeal to the LORD against you, and you will be found guilty of sin. [10]Give generously to him and do so without a grudging heart; then because of this the LORD your God will bless you in all your work and in everything you put your hand to.[18]

It is often convenient to avoid the poor, even if they are among us. The *Washington Post* explained that the Census Bureau's statistics on domestic want and deprivation has hardly shifted. "The 2005 poverty rate of 12 percent barely budged from the previous year's number."[19] The *Post* postulates that while poverty levels have not changed since 1973, the same level of poverty may not be accurate. "With more access to credit, greater income swings from year to year, and improved nutrition, housing, and health care, the life of America's poor is radically different today. Unless the nation's basic poverty indicators take into account such new conditions, any effort to effectively redress poverty in America is bound to fail."[20] The government has failed to use new measures to adapt the numerous indicators that have evolved.

The dual challenge for middle-class Christians involves facing the reality of their wealth, while attempting to live modestly. Brueggemann writes, "Whether we are liberal or conservative, we must confess that the central problem of our lives is that we are torn apart by the conflict

17. Ibid., 69–70.
18. Deuteronomy 15: 9–10.
19. Eberstadt, "Why Poverty," The *Washington Post*, B–1.
20. Ibid.

between our attraction to the good news of God's abundance and the power of our belief in scarcity—a belief that makes us greedy, mean, and unneighborly. We spend our lives trying to sort out that ambiguity."[21]

THE NEW TESTAMENT CHURCH MODEL

The early church in the New Testament followed the equal distribution rule with force and rigidity.[22] The early Christians believed in the mission and advancement of the church. Like their ancestors in the Old Testament, they did not believe in gaining or getting if it meant that others around them remained poor.

Possessions are spiritually dangerous, and God's people must practice self-denial to aid the poor and share the gospel. But we must maintain a biblical balance. "It is not because food, clothes, wealth, and property are so inherently evil that Christians today must lower their standard of living. It is because others are starving."[23]

The crucial test is whether the prosperous are obeying God's command to bring justice to the oppressed. The connection between righteousness, prosperity, and concern for the poor is explicitly taught in scripture.[24]

> Happy are those who fear the Lord who greatly delight in his commandments . . . Wealth and riches are in their houses, . . . they are gracious, merciful, and righteous. It is well with those who deal generosity and lend, who conduct their affairs with justice . . . They have distributed freely, they have given to the poor. Psalms 112:1, 3–5, 9 (NRSV).

> Give me neither poverty nor riches; feed me with the food that is needful for me, lest I be full, and deny thee, and say, "Who is the Lord?" Or lest I be poor, and steal, and profane the name of my God. Proverbs 30:8–9 (KJV).

21. Brueggemann, "The liturgy of abundance," *Christian Century*, 343.
22. See Acts 2:43–47; 4:32–37; 5:1–11; 6:1–7.
23. Sider, *Rich Christians*, 101.
24. Ibid., 102.

THE EXAMPLE OF JESUS

An important role that Jesus had while on this earth was to restore equality. It was through His death and resurrection that we are able to have that hope for ourselves. Throughout the gospels, emphasis is placed on using wealth and abundance for assistance to the poor.

> [18]"The Spirit of the Lord is on me,
> because he has anointed me
> *to proclaim good news to the poor.*
> He has sent me to proclaim freedom for the prisoners
> and recovery of sight for the blind,
> to set the oppressed free,
> [19]to proclaim the year of the Lord's favor."
>
> Luke 4:18–19[25]

Sider writes, "God wants us to create wealth and delight in the bounty of the material world. But historic Christianity also placed firm boundaries on this materialism. Nothing, not even the whole material world, matters as much as one's relationship with God. The Sabbath reminded people that once every seven days we should cease from work and focus on worshipping God. Happiness comes first of all, not from material things, but from right relationships with God and neighbor and from a generous sufficiency of material things.

Working harder to earn more money to buy ever-bigger houses and more sophisticated gadgets and cars has become a national passion. Regardless of the fact that 86 percent of Americans continue to tell pollsters that they believe in God, they have become practical materialists."[26]

BOLDNESS IS REQUIRED

Prophetic intervention requires boldness. Preachers today have a difficult task in conveying God's intention for justice. The "prosperity message" that has become popular among numerous evangelical congregations has blurred the understanding of God's intention for social action.

Walter Brueggemann argues for a less consumer-driven church, in favor of a community that serves as the mouthpiece for social justice, equality, and basic human rights. "The contemporary American church

25. Italics added for emphasis.
26. Sider, *The Scandal*, 88–89.

is so largely acculturated to the American ethos of consumerism that it has little power to believe or to act."[27]

The dynasties of the past set people up for failure. "The royal consciousness leads people to despair about the power to move toward a new life."[28] In reality, one must offer hope through what Brueggemann calls an "alternative prophetic community." This community must be energized through the collective consciousness of faith. The task of the prophet is to help the people imagine what life could look like ideally. In the corporate and prophetic world, this is called vision. "The prophet seeks only to spark the imagination of this people, and that in itself turns despair to energy."[29] This "imagination" sets the tone for what may be possible.

Jesus came to the earth to reclaim the original mission of Moses. Unlike the imperialistic leanings of Solomon and other kings, Jesus came to dismantle the historical misunderstanding of truth. His purpose was to breathe new life, by energizing people to a better way of living. Through Jesus' poverty, hunger, and grieving he taught the importance of loving others rather than ourselves.

Moses' intention was to lead the people out of the consumer-driven society in which they had been enslaved and into a new way of living. This new paradigm would be driven by faithful acts of kindness, love, and generosity. Unfortunately, God's people quickly became absorbed with the past and failed to live in harmony.

The challenge for today's thoughtful Christian is to embrace the alternative prophetic community. How can we live a faithful lifestyle that does not contradict our Christian values? Prophetic boldness requires action.

How is the enemy of materialism affecting your church ministry? How can your church brand be reshaped by confronting this enemy?

27. Brueggemann, *The Prophetic Imagination*, 1.
28. Ibid., 59.
29. Ibid., 77.

9

Viral v. Paper

Identity Crisis in the Church

It's amazing that the amount of news that happens in the world every day always just exactly fits the newspaper.

—Jerry Seinfeld (1954–)

THE CHURCH IS FACING a monumental crisis in conveying its message. A chasm is being forged between the religious community and secular society, due to rapidly changing technology. The ability to communicate the message through all forms of media may be the greatest hindrance in brand development for the church.

INFORMATION SHARING

On January 1, 2007, the world's oldest newspaper still in circulation, *Post-och Inrikes Tidningar*, dropped its paper edition, and became available only through the Web. "We think it's a cultural disaster," says Hans Holm, who served as the chief editor of *Post-och Inrikes Tidningar* for twenty years. "It is sad when you have worked with it for so long and it has been around for so long."[1] This caused ripple waves within the media community. The long, downward spiral of traditional print companies is forcing the closure of established institutions.

Malcolm Gladwell writes in *The Tipping Point* about social epidemics—how ideas, messages, and products can become contagious. Borrowing from the field of epidemiology, he writes, "The Tipping Point

1. Ritter, "World's Oldest," www.yahoo.com.

is the moment of critical mass, the threshold, and the boiling point."[2] He identifies several types of people who are instrumental in getting the message to tip over and gain unstoppable momentum: connectors, mavens, and salesmen. Each has his or her part in the tipping system. Gladwell's book, published in 2000, was already on the cusp of becoming outdated due to a new medium: the Internet.

The rapid exchange of information shared through viral videos, Web sites, blogs, file sharing, and online news organizations, exemplifies the technological advances fueling the widening gap between church and culture. This influence has impacted the Christian church. It has forced the church to reconsider its methods of communication.

The Internet exploded into a massive informational network; it became a forum for ideas, messages, and product development.[3] "In 1991 the World Wide Web debuted, instantly bringing order and clarity to the chaos that was cyberspace," writes Thomas L. Friedman. "From that moment on, the Web and the Internet grew as one, often at exponential rates. Within five years, the number of Internet users jumped from six hundred thousand to forty million. At one point, it was doubling every fifty-three days."[4]

The popularity and growth catapulted the Internet into homes, schools, and libraries—making it accessible anywhere, anytime. The power of the Internet has allowed the smallest company or an unknown individual to immediately turn into a virtual celebrity.

The Web obliterated traditional forms of information sharing. Hence, a free market of ideas exploded.

THE THREAT OF PAPER

For centuries paper has been the primary source of information gathering and sharing. Prior to paper, the spread of information was limited. It was restricted to cave walls, drawings, stone, or wood. In the early 1400s, Johannes Gensfleisch zur Laden zum Gutenberg developed a

2. Gladwell, *The Tipping Point*, 12.

3. The terms "Internet" and "World Wide Web" are often used interchangeably. However, they are two separate entities, working in cooperation with one another through a set of codes. The Internet can be thought of as a place with files and information, while the World Wide Web provides the avenue to process and move these files from computer to computer.

4. Friedman, *The World Is Flat*, 61.

method of printing from moveable type, leading to the invention of the modern day printing press. Scholar Elizabeth L. Eisenstein says the printing press eventually "ripped apart the social and structural fabric of life in Western Europe and reconnected it in new ways that gave shape to modern societal, cultural, familial, and industrial changes facing the Renaissance, the Reformation, and the scientific revolution."[5]

Gutenberg's printing press changed the world. The power of published material, in books, magazines, and journals has left an undeniable authoritative mark in society since the fifteenth century. Other modern inventions such as the radio, cassette, eight-track tapes, vinyl, and compact disks did not pose a threat to paper until the development of the television. Marshall McLuhan writes, "Our official culture is striving to force the new media to do the work of the old. These are difficult times because we are witnessing a clash of cataclysmic proportions between two great technologies."[6] The threat to paper had finally come.

Many churches are facing a technological dilemma. Ronald Heifetz and Marty Linsky offer valuable insight regarding adaptive and technical challenges.[7] They suggest leaders should be concerned with adaptive (or broad) changes rather than technical (or simple one-step) changes. Sources of information such as print, television, or the Internet govern the technical challenges, but these are only the means of transmitting the message. The adaptive challenge requires outside thinking and testing.

Church members today are stuck between the twelfth and twentieth century—sitting in pews, reading from hymnbooks, paying offering with checks, receiving the church newsletter by mail. So how should a church brand its message by using new forms of media?

At New Hope we are not immune to the challenges brought by the rapid change of digital technology. In 2006, we spent more than $6,000 on telephone book advertising. The telephone company sales representative made a convincing argument in support of the big yellow book. However, our own independent research has shown that the median age of a New Hope attendee is 26. These attendees are more likely to use the Internet to search for information than open the phone book. Thus, we have invested significantly more in online resources to reach our target audience.

5. Eisenstein, *The Printing Press.*

6. McLuhan, *Gutenberg Galaxy,* 91.

7. Heifetz and Linsky, *Leadership on the Line,* 14.

Churches like New Hope are in a transitional period, shifting between paper and viral. Should we continue to print paper brochures to
promote the various ministries of the church? Should we exclusively
promote all of our ministries and events via the Internet, despite the fact
that we will marginalize the small percentage of people who may not
have access to, or knowledge of the viral world?

THE CHURCH AND MEDIA

The American church is trying to remain relevant. How will the church
transmit its message in an age where Americans are reading less?[8] In
1998, George Barna forecasted, "Our research indicates that by 2010 we
will probably have 10 percent to 20 percent of the population relying
primarily or exclusively upon the Internet for its religious input. Those
people will never set foot on a church campus because their religious
and spiritual needs will be met through other means, including the
Internet."[9]

The Internet has grown from a one-dimensional tool into an interactive labyrinth. Insiders have considered the first decade of the web
as Web 1.0, a one-dimensional informational outpost. However, in the
last several years, Web 2.0 has emerged as an interactive community of
file sharers: Facebook, Twitter, Blogs, TiVo, MySpace, Podcasting, RSS
Feeds, YouTube, CyWorld, and Picassa Photo are all examples of the latest technological forms of communication. Tom Beaudoin suggests that
the Internet may be a safe place for Xers to explore spirituality, within
the confines of their own perimeters.

> Cyberspace highlights our own finitude, reminding us that we
> can never be fully cognizant of all that is happening. We are just
> solitary souls among the millions in cyberspace, exploring less
> than one hundredth of one percent of all that is out there. In this
> way, cyberspace illuminates our human limits. Yet it also mir-
> rors our desire for the infinite, the divine. Given the omniscient
> and omnipresent, which may be what the obsession with speed
> is all about theologically. To search for this fullness of presence,
> one that spans and unites the human and divine, is to operate in

8. According to a report by the National Education Association, over the last twenty
years, the number of Americans who have read a work of fiction in the previous year has
fallen by 17 percent. "Reading Less: Glimmers of Hope Shine Through NEA Report."
The San Diego Union-Tribune, July 17, 2004.

9. www.barna.org.

the field of a divine-human experience in which spirituality and technology intersect.[10]

This year, New Hope Church entered the viral world. Our Web site (www.lookingforachurch.org) has become more interactive. Web site visitors can register for events, give tithes and offerings online, and download sermons. The pastors have started blogging, providing opportunities for the community to dialogue and leave comments. Shane Hipps comments, "Electronic culture has broken down major walls as we extend ourselves in a global embrace. Under these conditions, the world undergoes a kind of implosion; the barriers of time and space are abolished, greatly diminishing the scale of our world—which leads to the phenomenon of the Global Village."[11] As technology transforms the world, it is imperative that the church communicate through new and innovative means to maximize these advances and promote its messages more quickly, more effectively, and more comprehensively to more people.

What is your church doing to stay connected in the digital age? How much do you rely on paper? How does your target audience gather information? How can you accommodate its communication trends?

10. Beaudoin, *Virtual Faith*, 87.
11. Hipps, *The Hidden Power*, 40.

10

Postmodernism's Effect

In every age there is a new development of truth, a message of God to the people of that generation, the old truths are essential; the new truth is not independent of the old, but an unfolding of it . . . He who rejects or neglects the new does not really comprehend the old. For him it loses its vital power and becomes but a lifeless form.

—ELLEN WHITE

Hierarchy and defined power are not what is important; what's critical is the availability of places for the exchange of energy.

—MARGARET WHEATLEY, *LEADERSHIP AND THE NEW SCIENCE*

POSTMODERNISM MAY BE THE single greatest influential factor on humanity in the last five hundred years. It has altered society's perception of truth. This single influence may be the colossal threat facing the church—the dichotomy between modernity, under which many churches have lived and ruled—and the emergence of postmodern thought that is now influencing the Christian church.

POSTMODERNISM'S INFLUENCE

Postmodernism refers to the "intellectual mood and cultural expressions that are becoming increasingly dominant in contemporary society."[1] Its greatest influence is the effect it has had on how truth is understood. Critics of postmodernism refer to the phenomenon as "truth decay." Truth was ascertained at one time by a systematic sequence of steps. Order was revered. Postmodernism rejects the emphasis of rational discovery through the scientific method, which led to the enlightenment

1. Grenz, *A Primer,* 12.

and intellectualism; this shaped the organization of thought, decision-making, and rationalization.[2] The understanding of truth in North America and other Western countries has metamorphosed in seismic ways.

Postmodernism's influence was originally witnessed through architecture, art, and writing. During the 1960s–90s the effects of postmodernism reached new heights. Television, movies, literature, and art all influenced this phenomenon that was slowly creeping into the mass consciousness.

Today the Newtonian approach of logical systems is no longer accepted as the only way to discern truth. Margaret Wheatley expressed this idea in her management book *Leadership and the New Science*, "Our concept of organizations is moving away from the mechanistic creations that flourished in the age of bureaucracy. We now speak in earnest of more fluid, organic structures, of boundary-less and seamless organizations."[3]

Sir Issac Newton's seventeenth-century influence on logic and organization was a monumental gain for the scientific world. His theory of proof dismantled the urge to depend on shamans, wizardry, magic, and move into a new age of reason. This influence trickled down to the religious community. Christianity was now deeply interested in explaining its faith too. To have faith only was no longer seen as acceptable or intellectual. All dimensions of the Christian faith demanded logical and reasoned explanations. This rationale led to strict linear thinking and a search for absolute truths.

POSTMODERNISM'S CHARACTERISTICS

The defining characteristics of postmodernism have been debated for decades. Some critics believe it is too early to conclude how it is shaping society. Others believe the postmodern era is already over, and Americans are now experiencing a post-secular or post-Christian enlightenment. While the debate has not yet reached a conclusion, I will discuss some markers that are widely agreed upon and how postmodernism is shaping the Christian faith.[4]

2. Ibid.

3. Wheatley, *Leadership*, 15.

4. These elements are extracted from James K. Hampton's "The Challenge of Postmodernism," *Youth Worker Journal* (January/February 1999): 18–24.

Postmodernism seeks preference rather than truth.

The influence of postmodernism has deconstructed the notion of a single truth. Truth is now relative. In fact, postmodernism allows for many truths, a pluralistic concept that accommodates multiple views, thoughts, and traditions—all acceptable. Can many paths lead to one truth? Can many truths lead to one path? In other words, if something is working for you, then it must be the truth.

How is truth shaped? Modernists associated truth with law, principle, or a set of presuppositions. Can truth be limited to a set of words and grammar patterns in a sentence? Postmodernists would argue, "The word truth is simply a contingent creation of language, which has various uses in various cultures."[5] President Clinton's grand jury testimony concerning his affair with Monica Lewinsky drew attention to the details of truth. The omission of words, and his use of the English language to carefully craft sentences expressed a complex variation of truth. At the same time, the deconstruction of his testimony exhibited the complexities of truth ("It depends upon what the meaning of the word 'is' is . . ."). Postmodernism seeks community rather than the autonomous self.

Individualism is traded for shared community—valuing the group's collective contribution to truth, rather than oneself.[6] "In the modern era, power was understood as a relationship of authority. In the postmodern era, power is understood as an authority of relationships."[7] Relationships are critical. Eddie Gibbs describes Gen Xers' perspectives on absolute truth: "They are not interested in listening to people who presume to have all of the answers. Rather, they want to meet people who have a transforming relationship with God."[8] A personal experience with God is a greater witness than an intellectual diatribe on the subject. Postmodernism holds great value for human mystery over human process.

The scientific age and the industrial revolution catapulted technological milestones and advances in science. However, in the midst of human accomplishment, the mystery of the soul began to slowly fade. Postmodernism does not believe all of life's questions can be answered

5. Groothuis, *Truth Decay*, 92.

6. See Surowiecki, *The Wisdom of Crowds*. The author suggests that crowds, or group-think is more reliable than one person's opinion.

7. Sweet, *Soul Tsunami*, 166.

8. Gibbs, *ChurchNext*, 130.

through scientific rationalism. There still exists a great deal of mystery that we cannot understand.

Worship has become a tool to discover the mystery of God. "Worship steeped in revelation takes seriously the incarnation of Jesus Christ as a prophetic, pastoral, and priestly voice in dialogue with human experience. This worship honors sacrament as a mystery and moment of unity, among people of the spirit created in God's image."[9] Postmodernists are attracted by the mystery that surrounds worship. Postmodernism overlooks scientific discovery in favor of virtual reality.

Because everything cannot be proven through an outlined process, one must depend on his or her own feelings. Postmodernism gives credit to trusting one's senses (or feelings), rather than proving ideas through a systemic scientific process. "According to the postmodern appraisal, science cannot achieve its goal of expelling myth from the realm of knowledge."[10] Postmodernists dismiss the notion that knowledge is inherently good. They are suspicious that one truth can be the only option. They are looking for a personal experience. "Reason is not the sole means of gaining and judging knowledge. Since truth is non-rational, there are other means of discovering it, including emotions and intuition."[11]

Personal and shared experiences seem to matter more than mere facts. People are looking for relationships that matter deeply. A relationship is the key to a postmodernist's heart. The Newtonian approach that worked for modernists—in particular, Boomers—is rejected for real experiences that tell an authentic story. Postmodernism accepts moral relativism.

Postmodernists want choices rather than just one answer. They only trust what they touch or experience. "Truth is defined by each individual and the community of which each individual is a part."[12] They would rather express their doubt in God, than perpetuate a truth that they are questioning. Donald Miller articulates this expression of relativism in his book *Blue Like Jazz*:

> Every year or so I start pondering at how silly the whole God thing is. Every Christian knows they will deal with doubt. And they will. But when it comes it seems so very real and frighten-

9. MacLean, "Worship: Pilgrims in the Faith," *The Emerging Christian Way*, 183.

10. Grenz, *A Primer on Postmodernism*, 47.

11. Erickson, *Postmodernizing the Faith*, 87.

12. Hampton, "The Challenge of Postmodernism," *Youth Worker Journal* 18–24.

ing, as if your entire universe is going to fall apart. I remember a specific time when I was laying there in bed thinking about the absurdity of my belief. *God. Who believes in God? It all seems so very silly.*[13]

Postmodernism permits pluralistic theological beliefs.

A mix-and-match theology is permissible. A fusion of religious traditions can be experienced in worship. This concept can be best illustrated through Elizabeth Gilbert's bestselling book *Eat, Pray, Love.* After going through a divorce, Gilbert travels to Italy, India, and Indonesia in an effort to find herself. During her visit to India, she studies major world religions to determine how to live her life. Her quest for spiritual direction leads her to study Yoga, which has been associated with Eastern religious practices. The author illustrates how the practice of another religion is influencing Christianity and other world traditions:

> True Yoga neither competes with nor precludes any other religion. You may use your Yoga—your disciplined practices of sacred union— to get closer to Krishna, Jesus, Muhammad, Buddha or Yahweh. During my time at the Ashram, I met devotees who identified themselves as practicing Christians, Jews, Buddhists, Hindus, and even Muslims.[14]

The influence of postmodernism on religion is evident through the previous example. Wheatley suggests, "Hierarchy and defined power are not what is important; what's critical is the availability of places for the exchange of energy."[15] Pluralism is part of the Western landscape. "Powerful hegemonic voices in pluralism compete against each other with conflicting versions of truth and goodness."[16] Modernity would never permit the intermixing of religious ideas. As the world continues to become "flattened," the repercussions are felt on religion. Postmodernism is more concerned with human misery, than human progress.

The advances made by the industrial revolution permitted a small group (mainly Westerners) to experience wealth, power, and education. Postcolonialism gave an uneven advantage to some—allowing one group

---

13. Miller, *Blue Like Jazz*, 87. Italics added.

14. Gilbert, *Eat, Pray, Love*, 122.

15. Wheatley, *Leadership*, 72.

16. Shenk and Stutzman, *Practicing Truth*, 192.

to become more powerful. Dr. Mabiala Kenzo, a theologian, explained why he believes postmodernism is an ally of postcolonialism:

> Most non-Westerners seem to prefer to use the term postcolonialism to describe the struggle for identity in the non-Western cultural context today. Those non-Western thinkers who have embraced the notion of postcolonialism join hands with all those who, wherever they may be found, are seeking to come to terms with the experience of colonization and its aftermath. Postmodernism turns out to be an ally of postcolonialism in that those who are seeking to come to terms with the experience of colonization and its long-term effects see in postmodernism not only the possibility of an alternative discourse that affirms and celebrates otherness, but also a strategy for the "deconstruction of the concept, the authority, and assumed primacy of the category of the West."[17]

The excessive consumption of the rich has left the marginalized without a voice. A "survival of the fittest" attitude seems to reign, leaving poverty, disease, and misery as a viable option. Eddie Gibbs suggests that "contemporary evangelicalism is a growing desire for an authentic and rich experience of God, and for that experience to be related to a personal call to holiness and to service in the world."[18] Postmodernism rejects colonialism and is deeply concerned with the human condition. Attention is given to issues in the wider world, instead of focusing exclusively on local community. While past generations such as the builders and boomers have traditionally leveraged their finances with building churches (a shrine to ourselves), a younger generation, heavily influenced by a postmodern, postcolonized world, wants to leverage its wealth in social causes.

Postmodernism has the potential to retell the story of social justice. Brian McLaren writes, " . . . we are emerging into a postmodern faith, a post-Western faith—not a faith that wants to forget and deny the many blessings of Christian faith in Western idioms, but a faith that no longer wants to be in denial about the dark sides of our history. We are emerging into a new era of Christian faith as a 'living color' global community, from a religion of conquest and control to a faith of collaborative mis-

---

17. Kenzo, "Evangelical Faith & (Postmodern) Others," originally quoted by McLaren, "Church Emerging," *Prism*, 2007.

18. Gibbs, *ChurchNext*, 144.

sion and humble service."[19] Postmodernism is devoutly concerned with helping others in need, even if it means losing power for ourselves.

Humanitarian campaigns have been tugging at the heart of postmodernists who care deeply about social issues. The advent of the "Red" campaign led by U2 superstar Bono has largely profited due to Gen Xers and Millennials. They believe they are supporting a cause while benefiting personally from shopping and feeding their own consumerist tendencies. While modernists would align their giving with tried and tested nonprofits such as the United Way or Red Cross, postmodernists are weary of the big organizations that may be too bloated and unwieldy to make an impact. They are more willing to take a risk with streamlined start-up groups that have a targeted project that they can support.

GENERATIONAL SIMILARITIES

Generations X and Y are the first generations to grow up under the matrix of postmodernism. They are less interested in the scientific method associated with builders and boomers. Michael Slaughter says in *Unlearning Church* that this new generation is pursuing church as an experience.[20] The younger generation believes that spirituality requires a certain degree of faith and mystery.

THE DILEMMA

The history of the Christian church is deeply rooted in modernism. Its beginnings and evangelistic tools can be best described through the scientific method and an empirical approach. The church has used extrinsic proof as its primary tool to convince nonbelievers to obey the rules that govern it. How will the church rebrand its message to reach the world in a postmodern and post-secular context?

THE NORTH AMERICAN ADVENTIST CHURCH

In order to describe the seriousness of this issue, I will highlight my own denomination's challenge. I write this, not to show fault, but rather to demonstrate the far-reaching effects of postmodernism, and how it is even influencing fundamental denominations such as the Seventh-day

19. McLaren, "Church Emerging," *Prism*, 2007.
20. See Slaughter, *Unlearning Church*, 36–41.

Adventist Church. An example from my denomination may serve as a microcosm of what is happening in the larger Protestant church.

The worldwide Adventist church is growing at astonishing rates. The Inter-America Division of the church celebrated its three millionth member in 2006. There are more than 15 million Seventh-day Adventists around the globe. However, the church in North America is not growing overall.

The effects of postmodernism as witnessed in England during the last fifty years are now similarly creating a post-secular society in America. According to a 1999 article, 89 percent of Britons do not go to church regularly, and the Archbishop of Canterbury has proclaimed the Church of England "one generation away from extinction." In France, only 3–4 percent of Parisians regularly attended church in 1998. In Norway, only 4 percent did.[21]

The dramatic religious shift seen in England in recent years may represent the climate that is now sweeping through the United States. While England has had a high immigration rate over the last twenty years, similar to the United States, 95 percent of the British population is still made up of English-speaking Whites. Of the twenty thousand Adventists in that country, about 10 percent reflect this majority. But of the eight thousand Adventists in London, only about one hundred are White.[22] The Adventist church in England has a serious problem with retaining English-speaking Whites. This is reflective of what is happening in North America today. If it were not for the immigrant churches in America, Adventism would be losing members in North America. Jon Paulien argues, "When it comes to evangelism, we do not face a racial problem but an indigenous problem."[23] The effect of postmodernism is transformation, which is characteristic of the traditional colonization many indigenous Christians lived under.

The retention rate in the Adventist church is low. For every two new members joining the Adventist church in North America, someone is dropped from membership. Those leaving the denomination are not new converts, rather they are young adults who grew up in the church.

---

21. Power, "Lost in Silent Prayer," *Newsweek*, 50–55. Quoted by Rice, *Believing, Behaving, Belonging.*

22. Paulien, "God's Mighty," *Ministry*, 10.

23. Ibid.

There are several factors that are causing this crisis in the American Adventist church.

The church is growing older. The median age of an attendee at a Seventh-day Adventist Church in North America is age 57. The median age in the United States is 37. As a result, the deep-seated traditions of modernism, which accompany many boomers, is clearly evident in the culture of the church and how it is led.

It is clear that taking the modernistic approach in evangelism and creating relevancy for seekers is not effective among postmodernists. The church must change its approach or fade into obscurity in North America. I will briefly examine two other critical issues facing the denomination as it relates to postmodernism.

GRACE ORIENTATION

Since its inception, the Seventh-day Adventist Church has been conflicted over a long-standing internal argument about justification by faith. To prove their point, many traditionalists have quoted one of the church's founders, Ellen White: "Those who accept the Savior . . . should never be taught to say or to feel that they are saved."[24] Others argue that her words were taken out of context. Yet this leaves many Adventists unsure of their salvation, leading them erroneously to seek salvation by works.

The earliest and most prevalent example of this is evident in the Adventist belief in the Sabbath. Adventists have been passionate about "proving" that the seventh-day Sabbath is still relevant, and must be observed. The weight of this issue is so paramount that it is even included in the official name of the denomination, "Seventh-day" Adventist. The church has used linear methodology to persuade people (mostly other Christians) of the Sabbath's empirical "truth." But proving a truth is not as important to postmodernists as experiencing it.

In 1989 the Adventist church commissioned a study of its young people. It was the largest and most comprehensive denominational study of church youth. It assessed their faith and values in the context of the most influential institutions: family, church, and school. It was undertaken to identify what about those venues encouraged a mature

24. White, *Christ's Object Lessons*, 155. Quoted by Weber, *Adventist Hot Potatoes*, 26.

faith and positive values development.[25] This monumental study of children and teenagers attending Adventist parochial schools was called *Valuegenesis*. Ten years later, another study, *Valuegenesis,[2]* was commissioned to compare two generations and determine if any changes were apparent.

The results in both surveys were staggering for denominational leaders. The impact of the study set in motion a whole series of events that resulted in more effective ways to help youth toward a life of commitment and loyalty to the Adventist church. The study offered insights on how young people were feeling, and revealed specific areas where leaders and educators needed to focus their efforts. One of those areas was grace orientation.

Grace orientation is a foundational truth that young people must comprehend in order to experience their faith. This topic affects how people view their own worthiness in relationship with God. The surveys found a high percentage of young people were unsure of whether they were saved.

Many of the young people did not understand that salvation was a free gift, and that there wasn't anything (including good deeds or following a set of rules such as the ten commandments) that could earn them their eternity. Sixty-five percent of the Valuegenesis[1] respondents said, "The gift of salvation is free, but you must keep the law to be worthy of salvation." Ten years later 53 percent agreed with the statement. When asked, "To be saved you must try to live by God's rules," 85 percent of the Valuegenesis[1] respondents agreed with the statement, however after ten years, only 74 percent of the Valuegenesis[2] agreed. The study also revealed that as students grew older and their faith matured, they developed a better understanding of grace.

The misunderstanding of grace among Adventist young people attending parochial schools helped illustrate the wider issue facing the church. The issue of salvation has led the church in the wrong direction, missing the beauty of the grace message.

One of the most common evangelistic techniques among Seventh-day Adventists has been proving why one must obey the Sabbath in or-

---

25. The Valuegenesis survey was overseen by the John Hancock Center for Youth and Family Ministries at La Sierra University, Riverside, California. The survey was funded by the Seventh-day Adventist denomination. To download the survey results and commentary, visit http://www.lasierra.edu/centers/hcym/.

der to gain God's attention. Many Adventists have made the Sabbath a criterion for salvation. This technique is a good example of a Newtonian approach, where order dictates the reality. Adventists living under the postmodern influence will need to define a new paradigm of understanding (and obeying) God through relationships, experience, and personal identity.

IDENTITY

The Adventist identity is a highly complex matrix. Born out of the Anabaptist movement, the church was founded on issues opposing the Methodist movement, mainly the seventh-day Sabbath. As Julius Nam writes, the defining characteristic of Adventism "is not any one doctrine or collection of Scripture. This is a certain *attitude toward* being a community."[26] The internal culture, which exists within the church, is built on stories, recipes, unique church speak, and networking—all of which help build the strong ties of identity for members.

Just as branding helps with corporate identity, it also helps the consumer (member) know where he or she fits within the institution. Good branding creates a place where people can belong. It inspires and invites consumers to feel they are welcome. "At its core, a brand is not the appearance of packaging or the humor of commercials. A brand is how people experience the values of an organization. Great experiences inspire loyalty and community."[27]

The need to belong is enormous. To belong means one is part of a larger community. Personal involvement and contribution to the community is valued. Richard Rice contends that Judaism's sense of community is part of its unique tradition. The tradition has three basic elements; believing, behaving, and belonging. "To be a Jew is first and foremost to belong to the Jewish community, to connect your life to the life of the community, to make the community a central part of your own identity. On a second level, it involves observing the community's traditions of worship, following the community's way of life. Then, perhaps on a third level, it involves believing—accepting the truth of certain doctrines."[28] Rice suggests community is more important than ethos.

26. Nam, "Adventism in Present," Adventist Today, September 2007, 8.

27. Salzman, "The New Stewards," Mid-America Outlook, July 2007, 6.

28. Rice, Believing, Behaving, Belonging. I sat next to Dr. Rice on a long flight from Israel to Los Angeles in 1999. Much of this section comes from my conversation with

Jews—unlike any other people group—cannot be defined by their ethnicity, race, religious orientation, or language. Therefore, how do they engender community? Rice notes that every Jew knows that he or she belongs to the wider community first, even before announcing whether he or she believes in all of the doctrines and practices of the community.

Has the Adventist church (and the greater Protestant church) focused on believing before belonging? Historically the church placed a heavy emphasis on believing the doctrines, (i.e., Sabbath, remnant, etc.) and behavior modification (vegetarianism, no smoking, no drinking, etc.), often at the price of community. The Seventh-day Adventist Church has often been known for what it stands against, rather than as a loving, caring community. What does the brand message say about this denomination?

Young people in the church did not feel that the church was a safe place to grow and be respected. Church sociologists believe "climate issues" are critical for future church retention rates. Most people leave the church over climate issues rather than doctrinal ones. According to the Valuegenesis[2] survey, only 40 percent of the respondents felt that church is a "place where they can think and grow and is open to new ideas and encourages questions." And only 59 percent of the Valuegenesis[2] respondents agreed with the statement: "My teachers or adult leaders care about me." This is startling, compared to the 79 percent of the mainline youth and 82 percent of the Southern Baptist who answered the same question differently. The report sums up with the statement: "We have some local work to do here!"[29]

Community is a popular buzzword used in postmodern circles. Xers and Millennials strive for authentic relationships, and community (*koinonia*) remains a foundation of the early church. "If Christian communities can learn to experience the kind of community the New Testament proclaims, they would find postmoderns quite interested in what they have to offer."[30] The local church must endeavor to welcome every person in the community equally.

The Seventh-day Adventist church has an enormous responsibility to share the saving story of Jesus. Unfortunately, the branding message

him, as he was writing this book.

29. Valuegenesis[2] study; see update 6, June 2002.

30. Paulien, "God's Mighty," *Ministry*, 12.

has been convoluted. Some believe the message should be about the Adventist distinctives, while others believe it should be the redemption story of Jesus. As the church finds ways to market itself, it is apparent that one unifying message should be considered.

People easily gravitate toward religious groups that have an air of exclusivity and claim to have a special message from God. The Adventist church has historically believed itself to have a special message from God. "Adventism, like Israel, has received a special calling from God. We can fail if we do not live as God wants us to be. Still, in the end, God removed them from their privileged position because of their repeated failures to live up to the covenant."[31]

How can the church develop new structures that will enable a better mechanism for communicating its message? The globalization of the world has flattened the organizational structure.[32] This will require a clearer understanding of the cultural context. Jan Paulsen, president of the global church wrote, "Contextualization, by which I simply mean making the message culturally appropriate, is an inevitable process. None of us is asked to step out of our own culture to become an Adventist. It is through our culture and our history that we experience life, and this cannot, and should not, be shed. So, within proper limits, contextualization must happen."[33]

Postmodernism accepts contextualization. In order to be relevant, one must examine and understand the context of the culture. If the Adventist church is to survive, it too must deconstruct modernity, which pervades the church, and reconstruct a message that can be adapted to postmodern thinkers.

Jon Paulien has argued that the church must speak and live in the language of society.[34] Truth must come in a form that people can understand. Just as the New Testament was written in the everyday language of Greek, (as opposed to the language of many scholars, which was believed to be "heavenly" because it was incomprehensible, compared to the public records of the government and law), so too must the contemporary Christian church contextualize its faith to reach the masses.

31. Bradford, "Warning from Ancient Israel," *Adventist Today*, 12–13.

32. See Friedman, *The World Is Flat*, 504–14.

33. Paulsen, "The Openness," *Adventist World-NAD*, 8.

34. Paulien, "God's Mighty," *Ministry*, 18.

The church has become self-centered. It has placed a priority on subjects that may be meaningful to believers, instead of focusing on the needs of secular people. Topics such as the nature of Christ, original sin, authority of the Bible are all popular subjects, however these may not appeal to the social needs of secular people. Bertil Wiklander argues, "The church could fulfill its Christian mission by finding a way to listen to these silent needs of secular people."[35] Secular people are interested in social causes bigger than themselves, such as the environment, hunger, genocide, and social justice. And frankly these are all topics that Jesus concerned Himself with as well, both in the Old and New Testaments.

How is postmodernism influencing your church? How is your brand being threatened by the effects of postmodernism?

The critical issues facing the church must be addressed if the church is to remain vital and healthy. These four issues facing New Hope—the multicultural clash, consumerism, the emergence of viral communication, and the postmodern influence in the Christian faith—should be considered when developing a brand strategy. Brand managers must intuitively recognize that any one issue could inhibit church growth. These four critical issues require New Hope's careful review as the church develops its strategic plan.

35. See Wiklander, "Understanding Secular Minds," *Ministry*, 12–15.

Part Three

11

Contextualization

Why do you yourselves transgress the commandment of God or the sake of your tradition?"

—JESUS CHRIST, MATTHEW 15:3 NASB

The goal is not to Christianize Africa, but rather to Africanize Christianity."

—UNKNOWN MISSIONARY

IN 1992 I WALKED into the chaplain's office at my Christian college and said to the lady sitting at the front desk, "Hi, I'm Kumar, and I want to be a student missionary."

"Well, what do you have in mind?" Nancy asked as she stood up and picked up the call book. The call book was a listing of more than eight hundred missionary positions available for students in my denomination. These positions gave students an opportunity to take a year off from school and serve in some kind of capacity, anywhere around the world.

"Well, I don't want to go to the usual places like most student missionaries. I don't want to go to an exotic island and be stuck teaching English as a second language. I want to have a real missionary experience in a rugged, remote place."

My optimism as an 18-year-old college student had grown after reading the book by Ellen G. White, *Acts of the Apostles*, in my dorm room. The life and journey of the apostle Paul had consumed my thoughts and I now imagined journeying across the globe to some remote place, telling people about Jesus for the first time.

"So you are looking for a real adventure, huh?" she asked.

"Yes, exactly, like a frontier experience," I announced with the un-bridled enthusiasm of the naïve.

She immediately closed the call book and looked straight into my eyes. "Did you say, 'frontier?'" she questioned.

"Yes," I said with slight hesitation. She had a weird look in her eyes. Why was she closing the call book? Did I offend her? Did she think I was kidding?

She walked around to the front of her desk and sat in the vacant padded guest chair next to me, "It is interesting that you said 'frontier.'" Her smile grew and her eyes widened as she told me about a mission outpost that sent missionaries to places around the world where the name of Jesus had never been uttered.

"You've got to be kidding," I exclaimed, I couldn't believe there were places in the world that still hadn't heard about Jesus.

"Believe it or not," Nancy responded, "there are many places in Papua New Guinea, Iran Jaya, and along the Amazon River where there are undiscovered people," she said as she handed me the student mis-sionary application to fill out.

I was intrigued.

Nine months later, I was on an airplane to Papua New Guinea. It would take twenty-six hours by air, nine hours sitting in the back of a pickup truck, and twelve hours by motorboat before I reached the village of Arai, on the May River—a tributary of Sepik, the second longest river in the world.

The Iwam people had only been discovered one generation before by the outside world. According to legend, small companies of Australian scouts were exploring the river when they suddenly encountered a group of Iwam men who had just completed a cannibalistic raid in a neigh-boring village. There was little interaction with the tribe thereafter, and during the next forty years very little would change along the May River. [Shortly after living in the village called 'Arai,' I met a man named Mou from a neighboring village who was old enough to remember participat-ing in cannibalistic raids as a child. He told me that the triceps are the "sweetest" tasting part of the human body. I took his word for it.]

The Iwam still lived in the Stone Age. They used rustic items such as stone, bone, and wood as hardware tools. While they were familiar with the outside world, only a few ever ventured out on their own to discover if the rumors of the "city" were true. Most never returned to confirm the stories. The Iwam were not familiar with White people and had only been exposed to a few Seventh-day Adventist and New Tribe missionaries, and one Scandinavian anthropologist named Rudy who lived in a remote village up river.

The Iwam had poor fishing skills and they were even worse hunters. Consequently, they tilled the ground to produce vegetables and fruit. They made a starchy substance called "sac sac" from the pulp of the sago palm to eat as their main staple. The sago palm was the ultimate jungle resource. Every part of the tree was used. They built homes from the logs, crafted roof tile from the dried palm leaves, and made sac sac from the pulp.

While clothing was optional, it was customary for women to be topless, wearing grass skirts made from the same sago palm leaves. The men wore shorts given to them by missionaries. However, for special occasions, and in remote villages deep in the bush where I would ultimately visit, the men wore only penis gourds.

Spiritualism shaped the religious climate of the Iwam. The people were driven by an animistic culture that dictated their decisions. Animism is the belief that gods are in all living organisms. Animists believe that there are millions of gods—they exist in all animate and inanimate structures (trees, blades of grass, animals). To the Iwam, one can never be sure of his or her standing with the gods. That is why the culture values making sacrifices and leaving food offerings in the jungle.

How can a missionary reach a group of people who exhibit a very different set of values, traditions, and spiritual assumptions? This has been the challenge for mission leaders throughout time. Clearly, traditional evangelistic methods that are successful in the West will not be effective within this cultural setting. The stories, metaphors, and illustrations would be too foreign for the Iwam to relate to. How do you convey the story of Jesus Christ in terms that your audience can understand? That was my dilemma.

Living in Papua New Guinea was a life-changing experience for me—one that ultimately shaped the way I approach ministry. As an 18-year-old, I was completely unprepared for the reality of life in the jungle. Upon arriving in my village, I hauled two large suitcases filled with toiletries, shampoo, bars of soap, candy bars, picture frames, magazines, cameras, camcorder, and every conceivable luxury item. I was prepared for missionary life in Europe, not the jungle! Even though the living conditions in Papua New Guinea had been explained to me over and over, it still didn't fully dawn on me until I showed up in the village for the first time and was forced to face reality.

I wasn't prepared to take baths every day in the crocodile-infested river, in front of the entire village—I expected some kind of privacy. I couldn't imagine that I was going to be catching my own rainwater. I didn't know that I was going to be digging my own outhouse during my first month. I hadn't taken into account that there wasn't anyone in my village who owned more than two shirts or pants. As a result, I left all of my brand new clothes hidden in a suitcase so I wouldn't insult the villagers or stand out in the crowd, and limited my attire to only two pairs of clothes for the rest of the year.

During my three-week mission orientation, I learned the importance of cultural assimilation. In order to present the gospel within the existing culture, we would need to live like the aborigines. This meant learning the language, using the same transportation methods (canoes), eating the same food, living in similar houses, and working side by side with the people. By immersing ourselves into an existing culture, we can discover commonalities with which to share the gospel in the framework of that culture. Missionaries call this contextualization.

In past generations, many missionaries failed to utilize the existing culture and beliefs to share Jesus. Missionaries with good intentions tried to share the story of Jesus from the only framework they knew, that of the Western world. Unfortunately, this often turned converts into "unintentional Westerners" whose adopted beliefs had little to do with the gospel. As a result, self-hatred and anti-nationalism were a common byproduct of evangelistic efforts worldwide. Anything that resembled the motherland was considered to be "native" or "unchristian." Moreover, in many cases colonialism created internal social problems, such as reverse racism or classism.

My parents are products of the influence of missionaries who carried out their work without carefully considering the culture and context. When the denominational missionaries first came to Southern India, they followed a process of evangelism using techniques of assimilation mandated since the days of William Carey, India's first missionary from the West.

These well-meaning missionaries and other colonists created an elitist system, thereby establishing a division between the missionaries and the very people they were trying to convert. The missionaries built elaborate mansions reminiscent of the Victorian homes they left behind in America and England. These homes were built on hills that over-looked the homes of the indigenous people, with protective high fences designed to shield the missionaries from any envisioned savage criminal acts. The compound was also staffed with a multitude of servants who were paid handsomely with cash and gifts by the Western missionaries. The money and gifts often inadvertently provided the indigenous popu-lation with persuasive motivation to brand-switch to Christianity.

The missionaries taught the people to read and write in English and established English schools throughout the countryside. They taught Western values as part of the curriculum and frowned upon anything that was remotely associated with the Indian race. whether it be lan-guage, music, dancing, clothing, certain foods, traditions, or folklore. "In this situation the sign system in the local culture has been so weak-ened that the sign system of the invading culture takes over completely, replacing the local sign system."[1]

In many respects, native people were reprogrammed into Westerners, often in completely inappropriate and ridiculous ways. For example, men living in sub-Saharan Africa were taught to wear heavy wool suits and ties to church in order to show respect for God, despite temperatures of more than 100°F.

CONTEXTUALIZATION

Contextualization has been a buzzword among missiologists during the last century. The concept grew in popularity as a result of some of the failures that took place in the mission field. During the previous two cen-turies, missionaries often shared the message of Jesus Christ by colonizing the converts. As Robert J. Schreiter contends, "In many parts of the world, expatriates have for too long dominated local communities, keeping them (often unwittingly) in a dependent position."[2] While this effect was not always intentional, it left behind long-term cultural damage.

Today international missionaries have made tremendous efforts to contextualize the gospel based on the existing culture. From my own

---

1. Schreiter, *Constructing Local Theologies,* 154.
2. Schreiter, *Constructing Local Theologies,* 19.

experiences in Papua New Guinea, I can see that this is a more effective method of bringing God's truth to people of differing cultures.

NORTH AMERICAN MISSIONS

Just as mission-minded leaders must attempt to share the gospel in relevant ways in other parts of the world, the North American church must do so now within its context. Yet the church has failed to adapt to the culture in relevant ways while still holding true to fundamental Christian principles. Simply put, if our brand lacks relevance, we have lost our effectiveness to make an impact in our community. A brand is only as good as its message. That is why the message must be transformative.

The church in North America has been aware of a decline in attendance for decades, but has failed to address the core issues. While we have been alarmed by the dwindling numbers, for decades we reassured ourselves with statistics that offered a glimmer of hope: "By many measures, Americans are strongly religious: 92 percent believe in God, 74 percent believe in life after death and 63 percent say their respective scriptures are the word of God."[3] Even though Americans were attending church less, they still believed in God and admitted to praying regularly.

Over the last decade a monumental shift has taken place, however. Americans are no longer placing their allegiance in a (monotheistic) God. In fact the influence religion has had on a person's worldview (politics, decision making, moral, etc.) is waning more than ever. In a *Newsweek* cover story, "The End of Christian America," the author points to the startling fact that "the number of Americans who claim no religious affiliation has nearly doubled since 1990, rising from 8 to 15 percent."[4] The number of people describing themselves as atheist or agnostic has quadrupled from one million to 3.6 million between 1990–2009.[5]

What has happened? Why is our self-described "Christian nation" evolving into a post-Christian state?[6] The president of the Southern

3. "Religious Americans: My faith isn't the only way," The *Associated Press*, http://www.msnbc.msn.com/id/25334489/.

4. Meacham, "The End of Christian America," *Newsweek*, 34–37.

5. Ibid.

6. The term post-Christian doesn't necessarily mean that American's no longer believe in God, but rather their faith no longer has a strong influence on their politics, affiliations, or culture.

Baptist Theological Seminary, R. Albert Mohler Jr., made the following observation: "The most basic contours of American culture have been radically altered. The so-called Judeo-Christian consensus of the last millennium has given way to a post-modern, post-Christian, post-Western cultural crisis, which threatens the very heart of our culture. Clearly, there is a new narrative, a post-Christian narrative, that has animated large portions of this society."[7]

THE BOOK OF HEBREWS

The book of Hebrews provides a helpful example of the rebranding challenge that we are experiencing today. The early Christian church had experienced a great awakening (see Acts 2–6) that brought about enormous growth and investment among the early Christians. However, as time passed, the church lost its purpose and no longer shared a unified story (or brand) on which to hang its message. Therefore, its message had difficulty taking root. According to the writer of Hebrews, "They heard the gospel but it had no value to them..."[8] The purpose of the book of Hebrews was to revitalize the dying brand of Christianity. It was to inject the early followers to hang on to their story. Today, the gospel is presented week after week in our churches, and yet it often falls on deaf ears. Our presentation hardly moves our parishioners into action. Our efforts (as heroic as they are) have failed to grow healthy, sustainable churches.

Just because we are losing ground, doesn't mean we should give up. Hebrews 10:36 remind us, "You need to persevere so that when you have done the will of God, you will receive what he has promised." God has given us the opportunity to tell *his* story. Now we must figure out how to convey his love in compelling ways that are easy for a hurt and dying world to understand.

While the issues related to contextualization are still being debated in academic circles, these are some helpful points that we must learn if we are going to rebrand our message.

7. Meacham, "The End of Christian America," *Newsweek*, 34–37.

8. Hebrews 4:2.

UNDERSTANDING THE PROCESS OF
CONTEXTUALIZATION

Math teachers have always impressed me. They have the task of explaining abstract calculations to a diverse group of students. While the students come from a variety of backgrounds, the teacher must connect with each one by using illustrations. Exceptional teachers will explain an idea or equation in terms that are relevant to their students. For example, if a student is involved in a sport, the math teacher may use illustrations or analogies from that sport to express a certain mathematical concept. Contextualization means telling a story in a way that is relevant to your audience, enabling them to understand the concept within their familiar field of reference. When applied to Christianity, this makes the gospel more approachable and gives people the best chance of hearing the message we are conveying.

12

The Danger of Contextualization

THE PRACTICE OF BORROWING rituals and adapting them into new cultural contexts is called *syncretism*. The term derives from the study of the religious climate in the Mediterranean basin at the beginning of the Common Era. During this time, competing cults borrowed heavily from one another and were constantly reshaping themselves.

THE EVOLUTION OF YOGA

The evolution of Yoga within the church is one of the better modern day examples of syncretism within Christianity. Just as the Northern Kingdom borrowed cultic practices from neighboring cultures and religions, Americans are adopting religious practices from Eastern religions that diametrically oppose the tenets of the Christian faith.

I greeted a couple at church one weekend before the service began. They indicated that they had just come from working out at their local gym. "Yeah," the husband explained, "we are doing Yoga every Saturday before church. We feel it prepares us for a spiritual awakening . . ." This response is typical for a growing number of churches in the West. In fact, *Time* magazine wrote about the rising trend in an article called "Stretching for Jesus":

> The platform is an altar, the tinkly tune is praise music, and the practice is Christian yoga. Senarighi's class, called Yoga Devotion and taught in the main chapel of St. Andrew's Lutheran Church in Mahtomedi, Minn., is part of a fast-growing movement that seeks to retool the 5,000-year-old practice of yoga to fit Christ's teachings. From Phoenix, Ariz., to Pittsburgh, Pa., from Grand Rapids, Mich., to New York City, hundreds of Christian yoga classes are in session. A national association of Christian yoga teachers was started in July, and a slew of books and videos are

about to hit the market. But the very phrase stiffens yoga purists and some Christians—including a rather influential Catholic— who insist yoga cannot be separated from its Hindu roots.[1]

The influence of Eastern religions has been growing in the American West. Just as the Northern Kingdom (that the prophet Amos was exposing) adapted practices from other religions, Americans are following suit in our day. Yoga in its purist form is not exercise; nor is it a breathing method. Rather, it is a form of religious foreplay. It prepares the human—mind, body, and soul—to open its spirit to the celestial. Yoga cannot and should not be practiced without the connection of Hinduism. "Moreover, others argue, Hinduism is not like a recipe ingredient that can be extracted from Yoga. Subhas Tiwari, professor of Yoga philosophy and meditation at the Hindu University of America in Orlando, Florida says: 'Yoga is Hinduism.'"[2]

MEDITATION v. CONTEMPLATION

The sudden interest in Eastern religious practices clearly demonstrates the human desire to seek understanding. As religious pluralism influences those in the West, it must be noted that people are not giving up on spirituality, but rather on religion. There is a deep interest in the unknown, or the mystery of God—as compared to conventional religiosity. Even lifelong Christians are fed up with the traditional forms of church and are searching for a spiritual experience that turns them on to God. The experimentation that exists within Christian circles can lead lifelong followers of Jesus to borrow from other belief systems to presumably enrich their Christian practice.

The difference between meditation and contemplation is very subtle. In fact, most people are unable to fully comprehend the nuances, and the words are often used interchangeably. The purpose of meditation is to drain the soul of energy (negative or positive). It is about opening the soul and mind in order to clear it out. The idea of "emptying one's mind" is not Christian. The emptying of your mind allows non-Christian influences and forces to fill that void. By contrast, the Catholic church has taught Protestant Christians most of what we know about

1. Mullen, "Stretching for Jesus," http://www.time.com/time/magazine/article/0,9171,1098937,00.html.

2. Ibid.

Christian contemplation. The purpose of contemplation is not to empty one's mind and soul, but rather, to *fill* it with God's presence. In recent years, the ancient practices of Christian contemplation such as Lectio Divina, the Centering Prayer, and Prayer Labyrinths have been revived as modern Christians explore the mystery of God.

It is easy to see how ordinary individuals can be attracted to the elements of Yoga and attempt to synchronize them into their religious frameworks. But while branding attempts to share of the gospel story in the most relevant manner, it cannot violate the basic tenets of Christianity. This example of syncretism may also shed light on its dangers. In fact, the effects of pluralism have been pronounced. According to a Pew Forum on Religion and Public Life survey, most Americans don't believe their religion is the only way to eternal life. Indeed, 57 percent of evangelical church attendees "said they believe many religions can lead to eternal life, in conflict with traditional evangelical teachings."[3]

Contextualization borrows the themes and broader story lines from culture to teach a greater lesson. The difference between contextualization and syncretism is subtle. Both contextualization and syncretism have powerful attributes that can help brand the gospel message, however it is important to understand their functions and identify the dangers. Dale Goodson, a former missionary who lived in the jungles of Papua New Guinea, explains the nuances of both of these approaches:

> Contextualization refers to seeking gospel clarity and its appropriate application with new, foreign contexts. Both contextualization and syncretism form relationships between the gospel and culture. Because of this, the two are often confused. Here is the difference: Syncretism allows culture to rule this relationship. Contextualization allows Biblical teachings and principles to rule. Contextualization is actually the most powerful antidote to syncretism. It fights the confusion that syncretism thrives on by speaking and demonstrating the gospel so members of the receiving culture can clearly understand it. It then guides them to appropriate application within their local cultural context.[4]

In *Constructing Local Theologies*, Catholic scholar Robert J. Schreiter describes three variations of syncretism. The first kind of syncretism—between Christianity and West African religions—is widespread

---

3. "Religious Americans: My Faith isn't the only way." MSNBC.com.

4. Goodson, "Exchanging, Not Mixing," *Adventist Frontiers*, 16–19.

throughout the northeastern coast of South America and throughout many islands of the Caribbean. "Christian deity and saints are amalgamated into the Yoruba or Io pantheons and communicated along the lines of African rituals."[5] Because of the borrowing of Christian elements such as Catholic symbols of holy water, candles, and statues, there is a nominal affiliation to Christianity; but in fact, many followers take an inimical posture toward the Christian faith.

The second kind of syncretism includes a blend of Christian and non-Christian elements, but uses the framework of Christianity for its organization. Some examples include the African Independent Churches and the Rastafarians in Jamaica. Rastafarians believe Ras Tafari to be their leader and the chosen prophet of God. While incorporating the usage of many Christian traditions and symbols, Rastafarians differentiate themselves through their distinctive clothing, their use of marijuana as a religious sacrament, their dreadlocks, and their singular music style.

The third form of syncretism is highly selective in its appropriation of Christian elements. Schreiter suggests that some religions such as the *Shinko Shukyo* in Japan have a high regard for Jesus. In one particular cult, Jesus shares the same altar with Muhammad and Buddha.

When borrowing from other traditions, the original message or religion will not remain unchanged. Author Shane Hipps suggests that as the medium alters, so too will the message, "Whenever methods or media change, the message automatically changes along with them."[6] Brad Harper and Paul Louis Metzger suggest, "Culture is an arena from and to which God speaks, but also one that distorts God's self-revelation. So it is not only acceptable but also necessary that we bring popular culture and its symbols into the church, for through them God engages us, and we respond to him. But since culture's symbols can also distort both God's engagement and our response, we must be wary."[7]

A LESSON FROM AMOS

The Old Testament prophet Amos provides a glimpse of how syncretism works. In Amos 4, the prophet chastises the people of the Northern Kingdom for their involvement in corrupt worship practices. Considered to be a controversial passage, the Old Testament prophet encourages the people to "Go to Bethel and sin; go to Gilgal and sin yet more."

5. Schreiter, *Constructing Local Theologies*, 146.

6. See Hipps, *The Hidden Power of Electronic Culture*, 30.

7. Harper and Metzger, "Here We Are to Worship," *Christianity Today*, 33–35.

Bethel was the chief religious sanctuary of the Northern Kingdom. It had housed the ark of the covenant and was one of the cities in the circuit followed by Samuel in his work as a judge (1 Samuel 7:16). Shortly after the division of the two kingdoms, Bethel was established as a sanctuary by Jeroboam I to provide an alternative to the sanctuary in Jerusalem.[8] In the time of Amos, the city of Bethel was known as "the king's sanctuary" (7:13).

So what was the problem? From all appearances, Bethel *was* a holy place for Israel. What was the prophet talking about when he said, "Go to Bethel and sin?" A closer examination reveals the spiritual erosion taking place at Bethel. The Israelites were borrowing cultic worship practices from neighboring Canaanite religions and incorporating these secular traditions and rituals into their Yahwistic (monotheistic) religion.

I doubt the Israelites had bad intentions. They were trying to personalize God in a way that was relevant within their culture. But in the process they seem to have lost the fundamental tenets of truth. While their attempt to contextualize their relationship with God may have been innocent, it was not pleasing to him.

The dominant culture that surrounds us will always offer an alternative form of worship that is appealing. This is the challenge we face as we attempt to convey the gospel within the language of the people. This is also the challenge that Paul faced when he admonished:

> Do not conform any longer to the pattern of this world, but be transformed by the renewing of your mind. Then you will be able to test and approve what God's will is—his good, pleasing and perfect will. Romans 12:2

Living within the dominant culture without incorporating its competing ideologies into our own religious practices is a balancing act. The Northern Kingdom attemped to contextualize its faith, but fell prey to the trap of syncretism. Similarly, if we introduce new traditions and blend them with what we deem to be Christian, what emerges may be a sort of pluralistic concoction that is no longer Christian.

The rules of branding in the secular world allow the use of "outside" images to promote a corporate brand. However, when branding the Christian message, the preservation of the Christian narrative must be of great concern.

---

8. Gaebelein, ed. *The Expositor's Bible Commentary: Daniel*, Vol. 7.

The dominant culture is our guide to expressing our faith to our audience in relevant ways. This may be the single most important value in sharing the gospel—to make sense to your audience. However, the story of Jesus and our expression of worship must still make sense to the church.

WHERE DO WE DRAW THE LINE?

It is not surprising to observe some pastors and congregations going to extreme measures to gain media attention. In a media-saturated society, it can be difficult for churches to attract positive exposure in the media. Public scandals in the church receive full media coverage. But bake sales, harvest festivals, and feeding the poor (except for holidays) no longer draw media attention. Some churches have been creative or resorted to publicity stunts to get attention. Detroit's Greater Grace Church gained international press coverage when the congregation prayed for several U.S. automakers. Here is an excerpt from a national online automobile media source, entitled "Detroit church turns Sunday into SUV-day with prayer for auto industry."

> In some parts of the world, it's normal to take along saints or other holy images for a Procession to ask for rain, a good crop or other benefit. A similar idea caught the minds of people at Detroit's Greater Grace Church, where the pastor made a symbolic move on SUV-day Sunday to pray for the future of the car industry. The objects of prayer? Three hybrid SUVs: a Ford Escape, Chevy Tahoe, and Chrysler Aspen. The holy trinity joined the Rev. Charles Ellis on the altar while many employees from the auto industry sat in the pews. While using hybrids was a good idea, praying for sales of high-mileage passenger cars would have been a nice touch. We'll see if the big guy upstairs is listening to the Big Three. Something brought down gas prices, after all.[9]

There seems to be a growing number of churches that are willing to do anything to get their community's attention. The immediate question that arises is how far should a church go? Many church leaders often cite the well-known passage where the apostle Paul says, "To the weak I became weak, to win the weak. I have *become all things to all* men so that by all possible means I might save some. I do all this for the sake of the gospel, that I may share in its blessings."[10] What does it mean to be *all things*? Does "all things" mean anything goes?

---

9. Navarro, "Detroit church turns," See http://green.autoblog.com.

10. 1 Corinthians 9:22–23. Italics added.

13

Leveraging the Culture

*Our message must never change, but the way we deliver that message
must be constantly updated to reach each new generation.*

—RICK WARREN[1]

We do not "spin" the Christian message; we live it.

—DAVID KINNAMAN[2]

EATING WITH JARED

Do you like Subway sandwiches? Apparently, so do millions of other
consumers. In 2009, the Subway brand had almost thirty two thousand
stores in ninety-one countries. The January 2009 *Entrepreneur* magazine
lauded it as the number one franchise in America. The 2009 Zagat fast-
food survey named the brand as the number one overall provider of
"Healthy Options," "Best Service," as well as "Most Popular." This is all
very surprising for a company whose sales were flat in 1999. How did a
relatively unknown submarine sandwich shop brand itself as the healthy
option—an enemy of fast food—and see its sales spike 34 percent in two
years? The answer: one compelling story.

It is hard to eat at a Subway restaurant now without visualizing
Jared, a college student who weighed 425 pounds and wore XXXXXXL
shirts—the largest size available in big and tall stores. Jared's story of
transformation revolutionized the Subway brand, and simultaneously
reminded marketers and brand consultants of how valuable it is to have
a *story*. According to the authors of *Made to Stick*, Jared often chose his

1. Warren, "Evangelizing the 21st Century Culture." Pastors.com. Quoted in Hipps,
The Hidden Power, 29.

2. Kinnaman and Lyons, *UnChristian*, 209.

college courses based on the type of seats and desks available in the assigned classroom—there were some models in which he could not fit. His obesity prevented him from living a normal life. Many of the people in his life worried about the long-term health effects that could result from his obesity. Even his father, a general medical practitioner, admonished him for years about the dangers of obesity without any success. Nothing seemed to have an effect on him until one day Jared's roommate, a pre-med student, noticed Jared's swollen ankles. Jared suffered from edema, a condition where the body retains water and prevents the blood from circulating properly. This condition can lead to diabetes and early heart attacks.

Finally, Jared made a personal decision to slim down. He was impressed by the "7 under 6" campaign the Subway restaurants were promoting. He walked into a Subway restaurant and ordered a turkey club. He liked it so much he decided to begin eating at the shop twice a day, eventually personalizing his own sandwich, a foot-long for lunch and a six-inch for dinner.

After three months of what he dubbed the "Subway diet," Jared stepped on a weight scale. He had lost 100 pounds, just by eating at Subway twice a day and walking back and forth to the store. Eventually he would lose 245 pounds, following the Subway diet he concocted.

It is hard to believe it now, but Jared's story was almost overlooked as a national marketing strategy. In the late 1990s the Subway brand had spent millions of dollars on its "7 under 6" marketing campaign. They were offering seven sub sandwiches with less than six grams of fat. While this was a very healthy option, the catchy phrase didn't yield any noticeable growth in Subway's sales. When the Jared story was initially pitched to the Subway executives, they brushed it off as being similar to the marketing campaign that they had just attempted. That was true in a sense, since both campaigns were marketing a healthy option. However, the first one used dry statistics to sell a product, whereas the other used a compelling narrative to motivate the target audience.[3] Jared's story inspired many others who faced the battle of the bulge. Within the first year of telling the Jared story, Subway's sales jumped 18 percent, and another 16 percent the following year in 2001, while its competitors experienced a 7 percent average gain.

3. Heath and Heath, *Made to Stick*, 218–23.

Jared Fogle's transformation continues to be a compelling story. The American public has watched Jared fight to keep his weight off, get married, have children, and celebrate his ten-year anniversary on the Subway diet.

The Jared story can teach the church how to explain abstract concepts by using visuals and compelling stories. This is the power of contextualization—moving from the abstract to the concrete; filling the void with emotion and human experiences.

In order to rebrand the gospel, we need to include stories that illustrate needs found within the current culture. Many pastors struggle to be relevant within the changing culture. "Pop culture has permeated every community in America, and most around the globe, regardless of how big or small, urban or rural crowded or remote," says Tim Stevens, author of *Pop Goes the Church*, "The question is not, "Does pop culture have an influence?" The question is, "What am I going to do with it? How will I respond? What choice will I make?"[4] Staying on top of the popular culture that is influencing the trends and shaping our local community can be a daunting task for some. Too often we cloister ourselves in our offices and depend on outdated stories found in large compilations of sermon illustration books, rather than engaging with the culture around us. Rather than using the current culture to convey the gospel, we are hostages to our practices and traditions.

LEVERAGING THE CULTURE

Here is an example of how one pastor leveraged a national news story to reflect the culture. Pastor Jason McGavin,[5] a local pastor in my community, had been trying for years to begin a courageous dialogue regarding racial integration within his congregation. Over the course of five years, his congregation had slowly "darkened," as people came from a growing number of ethnicities that more accurately reflected the surrounding community. This issue was becoming a concern to some of the longstanding members of the congregation. "I am not a racist," said one member in the private quarters of the pastor's study. "I am just concerned that we are not going to be able to attract Caucasians in the near future." How could Pastor McGavin address the escalating tension

---

4. Stevens, *Pop Goes the Church*, 67.

5. Pseudonym.

within his congregation? He wanted to face the issue openly and head on, providing a forum for people to express their views in a respectful way. Yet how could he call for an open dialogue without creating an uncomfortable environment for all parties involved?

In July 2009, Cambridge police arrested Harvard professor Henry Louis Gates Jr., one of the nation's preeminent African-American scholars, in his own home. This incident became a high profile news story that ignited a national debate about racial profiling. "Gates told the officer that he was being targeted because 'I'm a black man in America.'"[6] The story escalated when, during a live press conference, President Barack Obama stated that the Boston police department "acted stupidly." Immediately, the country was torn in two. Some believed the police officers acted within their power to restrain Gates, who was allegedly exhibiting belligerent behavior. Others believed the esteemed professor was a victim of racial profiling and treated more harshly because of his skin color.

Pastor McGavin saw this incident as the perfect opportunity to begin a discussion on race and equality within his church family. "How should our congregation respond to diversity?" he asked. By using a current example of something that was on the consciousness of the nation, Pastor McGavin opened a dialogue about the biblical teachings on equality. Instead of focusing directly on his church, he used the larger situation across the nation to address a critical issue facing his church.

Pastor McGavin's story is still being written. While the church hasn't yet found a perfect "feel good" ending, the congregational leaders have been able to participate in constructive dialogue about the future of the church and how it might be impacted by diversity and growth. This might not have happened if Pastor McGavin hadn't utilized the existing story in the popular culture as leverage to begin a difficult conversation. Contextualization uses existing stories, metaphors, crises, and principles that govern the dominant culture to brand the gospel.

HOW HEALTH CARE REFORM
CREATED A SERMON SERIES

The national debate on health reform has sparked hostility on both sides. The debate grew especially heated when President Obama and other democratic leaders held town hall meetings within their congres-

---

6. Jan, "Harvard professor Gates arrested at Cambridge home." www. Boston.com.

sional districts to boost support for the bill. The intense antagonism of the Americans who showed up in mass numbers to oppose the health care bill surprised most people, including the news media.

Gianlucca Bruno, an innovative pastor in Mason, Ohio, decided to capitalize on the buzz surrounding the controversy by launching a new sermon series titled, "God's Health Care Reform." The series didn't address the political debate in detail, however it addressed the heart of the issue: health care. In the third installment of the series, Bruno posed the question: "Can Faith Improve Your Health?" This well-advertised sermon series was popular within his community, but it also conveyed to the surrounding community that this church was attuned to what people were talking about and had something to add to the discussion.

UNDERSTANDING CULTURE WITHIN CONTEXT

What is culture? Robert Lewis and Wayne Cordeiro explain, "Culture represents the intersection of three values you're to steward: God's kingdom agenda, who you are, and your unique setting."[7] In other words, culture is the way you interpret your life. Theologian Tom Beaudoin contends, "We express our religious interests, dreams, fears, hopes, and desires through popular culture. Religious expression is not cultural reality. Christian symbols were not pristinely dropped from the sky. As the incarnation so profoundly illustrates, God reveals himself in the common."[8] As pastors and church leaders, we must become cultural and spiritual anthropologists. To merely regurgitate what we learned in seminary is a lesson in futility. Moreover, it limits what God can do in and through us to reach our neighbors.

The greatest obstacle to contextualization is ego. It is much easier to tell the story from our perspective. However, as cultural missionaries, we must determine how culture, language, and climate are transforming our communities. Brad Harper and Paul Louis Metzger suggest, "The symbols of popular culture transmit the shared meanings by which a people understand themselves . . . There are no truly neutral symbols, images, or rituals in popular culture."[9] One of the greatest mistakes missionaries made in the last one hundred years was to introduce *their*

7. Lewis and Cordeiro, *Culture Shift*, 21.

8. Harper and Metzger, "Here We Are to Worship," *Christianity Today*, 33–35.

9. Ibid.

gospel—a Eurocentric presentation that unwittingly colonized their converts. Today we are repeating the same mistakes in the West by failing to be culturally relevant here at home. Many church leaders think cultural relevance is a buzz phrase synonymous with contemporary rock music, skinny jeans, and glitzy PowerPoint presentations. The truth is that being culturally relevant will mean something entirely different based on the city in which you are serving. You will need to adopt techniques and tools based on your unique demographic needs.

Many churches fail to adapt their message to the prevailing culture. There is an assumption that non-Christians will somehow figure out *our* culture, language, and story. Pearl S. Buck's classic literary book *The Good Earth* records an interesting encounter when the lead character, Wang Lung, is approached by a foreign missionary. The well-meaning missionary thrusts a gory picture of a crucified Christ upon the uneducated peasant farmer:

> Now Wang Lung had never in his youth or at any time learned the meaning of letters upon paper, and he could not, therefore, make anything out of such paper covered with black marks and pasted upon city gates or upon walls or sold by the handful or even given away. Twice had he had such paper given him.
>
> The first time it was given by a foreigner such as the one he had pulled unwittingly in his ricksha one day, only this one who gave him the paper was a man, very tall, and lean as a tree that has been blown by bitter winds. This man had eyes as blue as ice and a hairy face, and when he gave the paper to Wang Lung it was seen that his hands were also hairy and red-skinned. He had, moreover, a great nose projecting beyond his cheeks like a prow beyond the sides of a ship and Wang Lung although frightened to take anything from his hand was more frightened to refuse, seeing the man's strange eyes and fearful nose. He took what was thrust at him, then and when he had courage to look at it after the foreigner had passed on, he saw on the paper a picture of a man, white-skinned, who hung upon a crosspiece of wood. The man was without clothes except for a bit about his loins, and to all appearances he was dead, since his head drooped upon his shoulder and his eyes were closed above his bearded lips. Wang Lung looked at the pictured man in horror and with increasing interest. There were characters beneath, but of these he could make nothing.
>
> He carried the picture home at night and showed it to the old man. But he also could not read and they discussed its possible

meaning, Wang Lung and the old man and the two boys. The two
boys cried out in delight and horror,
    "And see the blood streaming out of his side!"
    And the old man said, "Surely this was a very evil man to be
thus hung."[10]

This simple story depicts the distorted message an illiterate farmer
received when he was given a pamphlet of a bloodstained Jesus without
the relevant context. Today, the vast majority of Americans are biblically
illiterate (this includes many of our parishioners). The story of Jesus has
been limited to pint-sized sound bites about a baby born in a stable and
a God who wants you to burn in hell for an eternity for the minor infrac-
tions you commit throughout your life.

   Branding requires telling God's story in today's language. Wang
Lung, the fictitious character, could not relate to the White Jesus, hanging on a wooden beam, because the story was unfamiliar. Today many
Christian churches still rely on ineffective methodologies such as mail-
ers to their surrounding communities without sharing the joy-filled
message of Jesus. Branding guru Mara Epstein says, "Branding is about
making meaning—taking the individual aspects of a product and turning them into more than a sum of their parts. It is about giving consumers something to think and feel about a product or service beyond its
physical attributes. It's about fulfilling a need; providing what marketers
call the benefit."[11] In Christian circles, we would define the product as
being the gospel of Jesus Christ. This is a life-changing product that we
believe every person on the planet should have. What is the best way to
transmit this story within *your* context?

   Recently a Seventh-day Adventist congregation mailed 414,445
copies of a book originally written in the nineteenth century to its
neighboring community.[12] While I don't doubt the pure intentions of

10. Buck, *The Good Earth*, 131–32.

11. Einstein, *Brands of Faith*, 70.

12. I have chosen to use my own denomination in this illustration, rather than
criticize one with which I am not associated. The Seventh-day Adventist Church is one
of the fastest growing denominations around the world. However, in North America
growth in the church has stalled. There are many reasons for this phenomenon; one in
particular is the denomination's failure to understand the issues related to postmodernism. Like many of our sister denominations, we are stuck using traditional forms of
evangelism that were effective three or four generations ago, but lack relevance today.
To rebrand our image, we must be willing to forego what hasn't been working, and take

this particular church, I would question the usefulness and methodology of their actions. The church distributed the message without giving thought to the context in which it would be received. The local pastor leading this initiative said of the endeavor, "This is a heaven-sent opportunity for the churches in the greater San Francisco area to take the gospel to every home in this great city through the mass mailing of the book. This faith venture has reached 414,445 homes with *one of the most powerful resources we have for evangelizing the world—the printed page.*"[13] This particular congregation invested $262,000 in this single evangelistic project. But to what end?

After studying the demographic profile of the San Francisco area and the neighboring communities surrounding this particular church, I would argue that "the printed page" is *not* an effective tool to reach this highly secularized, techno-savy population. In fact, according to the U.S. Department of Education, reading levels and the interest in printed media have dropped drastically. Less than one-third of 13-year-olds read daily—a 14 percent decline from twenty years earlier. Among 17-year-olds, the percentage of non-readers doubled over a twenty-year period, from 9 percent in 1984 to 19 percent in 2004.[14] On average, Americans between the ages of 15 to 24 spend almost two hours a day watching TV, but only seven minutes of their daily leisure time is spent reading.[15] Branding guru Mara Einstein clarifies the importance of having a demographic understanding of your community, "The marketing techniques referred to here include demographic assessments of the area surrounding the church, as well as the use of surveys and focus groups to evaluate changing religious preferences . . . [such as the level of] distaste for face-to-face evangelism, demand for intellectual challenge within the church context . . ."[16] What kind of response did this congregation yield for their $262,000? According to Trevan Osborn's blog, the church "reached" a mere 0.097 percent of homes in the target area—not really a statistically

---

the risk to experiment with innovative methods.

13. http://trevanosborn.blogspot.com. Italics added.

14. U.S. Department of Education, National Center for Education Statistics (NCES).

15. U.S. Department of Labor, Bureau of Labor Statistics, *American Time Use Survey* (2006).

16. Einstein, *Brands of Faith*, 71.

significant number. If you had $262,000 to spend on a single evangelism project, how would you use it?

This story illustrates the powerful role that demographics can play in understanding your community. Churches have limited resources—financial and human. "Sadly research studies have shown that marketing, as a conscious set of activities growing out of an articulated marketing philosophy, is absent in more than nine out of ten evangelical churches. Most churches, by marketing standards, are failures: that is, they are not maximizing their potential for profit (i.e., ministry gains)."[17] Understanding your target audience is imperative if you are going to invest finite resources in a specific methodology.

What would your brand of Christianity look like if it adapted the cultural nuances of your community's demographic profile? How would your community's stories, traditions, music, and mythology shape your presentation of the gospel?

LESSONS FROM FAST FOOD

Some of the world's most successful food chains are contextualizing their products. If you were to order a Kentucky Fried Chicken meal at the Heathrow airport in London, you might be surprised to see how many of the items on the menu board are British adaptations of what you might find in Kentucky, USA. During a visit to London, I was surprised to find samosas, the south Asian potato-filled pastry, on the menu board. Can you see the irony here? A restaurant that has branded its identity on the southern cuisine of Kentucky is selling samosas to attract the wider market of south Asians living in London! Similarly, Costco Wholesale recently announced that some of its locations would be offering bulgogi, a Korean staple, in its popular pizza food courts. Why? Costco has noticed the upturn of Asian members in certain markets. How can Kentucky Fried Chicken offer different options on their menu in different parts of the world and Costco sell bulgogi? Both are contextualizing their brands to suit their particular audiences.

---

17. Barna, *Marketing the Church*, 26–27. Quoted in Kenneson and Street, *Selling Out the Church*, 42.

Church growth guru Lyle Schaller asks, "Are your leaders willing to change the shape of the vessel that carries the Good News that Jesus Christ is Lord and Savior?"[18] One group of marketing advocates wrote:

> We believe that no organization or group has a message of such urgent and life-changing *content* as the message of faith in God. Yet most churches fail to use the *concepts and tools* which can enable them to effectively communicate to current and prospective members and donors, as well as other groups which need so desperately to hear this message.[19]

Churches have been slow to adopt principles related to branding. The words *marketing, advertising, branding,* and *public relations* have been questioned among skeptics and perceived to be vulgar among Christian leaders. According to secular standards, the Christian church has failed to keep up with tried and tested principles that create identity. Some people fear that if the church were to utilize "secular" principles it would compromise its position. Pollster George Barna suggests that we must always protect the message but have flexibility in the method by which it is transported:

> Unlike a secular organization, in which the product would be manufactured in accordance with the market assessment, the product of the Church has to remain constant. We cannot tinker with our product—how we describe the product, package it, and convey it to our target audience, yes,—but the product itself is, so to speak, sacred . . . Thus, while the Church does not have to worry about conceiving, shaping, producing, and revising a new product, we would do well to remind ourselves exactly what our product is and take every precaution to be certain that we are not in any way, shape, or form changing the product to suit our environment.[20]

While protecting the gospel message is critical, it is also important to note that the message alters with the medium. Mennonite author Shane Hipps provocatively argues that the message never remains the

---

18. Schaller, *Create Your Own Future!*, 133. Quoted in Kenneson and Street, *Selling Out the Church*, 29.

19. Winston, Stevens, and Loudon, *Marketing for Churches and Ministries*, ix; italics added. Quoted in Kenneson and Street, *Selling Out the Church*, 29.

20. Barna, *Marketing the Church*, 56. Quoted in Kenneson and Street, *Selling Out the Church*, 30.

same when the medium is altered. Hipps's written work is a careful analysis of the twentieth-century writer Marshall McLuhan, an early adopter of media experiments, who coined the phrase, "The medium is the message." Hipps articulates what most church leaders are afraid to admit: "The *forms* of media and technology—regardless of their *content*—cause profound changes in the church and culture . . . we stand oblivious to the hidden power of media."[21] Every time the message is carried, whether it is through the written letters of the apostle Paul, or preached from the lips of evangelist Billy Graham, it (the message) will be altered. "It is imperative we move beyond this paradigm and realize that our forms of media and technology are primary forces that cause changes in our philosophy, theology, culture, and ultimately the way we do church," Hipps contends.[22] The gospel will always be altered because it is being told from our lens of understanding.

BORROWING FROM OTHER CULTURES

How can we share the gospel in a new light, without losing the integrity it stands upon? This has been the constant challenge for the church—keeping the message "pure and unadulterated."[23] Is there even a "pure" form of Christianity? "Borrowing" is a term commonly used when characteristics from the present culture are used in contextualization. Upon closer examination, many of the traditions and theological doctrines of Christians were borrowed from other cultures. Schreiter suggests that the formation of common Christian doctrines such as eschatology, angelology, and demonology would not be complete without the Persian influence on Judaism. Where do the Christian feasts of the dead (*Todos Santos*, the Polish *Wiglia*) come from? Christianity, like other traditions, has a long history of absorbing elements from the cultures in which it lived: Hellenistic, Germanic, Celtic, Syrian influences.[24] These practices, now considered to be "sacred cows," were contextualized practices that held great meaning within a particular time and space. The practices became so intertwined within a cultural and religious context, they took on greater meaning within the Christian expression and were carried on

---

21. Hipps, *The Hidden Power of Electronic Culture*, 23. Italics added.

22. Ibid., 27.

23. Schreiter, *Constructing Local Theologies*, 144.

24. Ibid., 151.

to other locations as tradition. Practices of the Christian faith evolved over time based upon the contextual circumstances that surrounded the tradition.

Many of these practices are outlined in Frank Viola and George Barna's book *Pagan Christianity?* One example of a modern "sacred cow," considered to be of utmost importance in Christian worship, is the sermon. As Viola and Barna point out, the tradition of the sermon is not a biblical mandate. In fact, the practice of a sermon in a worship service was not a fixture in Old Testament tradition. While there are a few examples of teaching and preaching spattered throughout the Old Testament, it was not a common practice, especially during corporate worship.

Similarly, the New Testament examples of sermons were not a common practice. Jesus, for example did not regularly preach sermons to the same audience. His teachings took on contextual form, based on the situation and setting. While some would argue that the Sermon on the Mount is a perfect example of Jesus sermonizing, let us not forget that the title, "sermon," was introduced four hundred years after the teaching on the mount. Augustine is the first to be credited with giving the Matthew 5–7 account this title in his book, "The Lord's Sermon on the Mount," written approximately between 392 AD and 396 AD. Even with this book title, the term "Sermon on the Mount" was not fully adapted until the sixteenth century.[25] The New Testament is peppered with examples of sermons, especially in the book of Acts, however the apostolic preaching was sporadic. It was delivered on special occasions in order to deal with specific problems. It was extemporaneous and without rhetorical structure. It was most often dialogical rather than monological.[26]

So where did the post-apostolic Christians learn the art and practice of our modern day sermon? According to Viola and Barna, this ancient practice was derived from pagan Greek culture, namely the Sophists, who were expert debaters.

25. See Green, et al., *Dictionary of Jesus and the Gospels*, 736; and Douglas and Comfort, *Who's Who in Christian History*, 48.

26. Viola and Barna, *Pagan Christianity?*, 199. See also, Norrington, *To Preach or Not*, 7–12. Acts 2:14; 15:13–21, 32; 20:7–12, 17–35; 26:24–29. Thomson, *Preaching As Dialogue*, 3–8. Barclay, *Communicating the Gospel*, 34–35. Kreider, *Worship and Evangelism in Pre-Christendom*, 37.

They were masters at using emotional appeals, physical appearance, and clever language to "sell" their arguments.[27] In time,
the style, form, and oratorical skill of the sophists became more
prized than their accuracy.[28] This spawned a class of men who
became masters of fine phrases, "cultivating style for style's sake."
The truths they preached were abstract rather than truths that
were practiced in their own lives. They were experts at imitating
form rather than substance.[29]

The Hellenistic influence of preaching only demonstrates how convoluted our religious practices are in the Christian faith. As Viola and
Barna point out, much of what we consider to be "pure" fundamental
practices of the church have in fact been borrowed (i.e., order of service, church buildings and architecture, tithing and clergy salaries, etc.).
These practices were originally contextually based, however through the
centuries they were adopted and carried forward to other cultures.

Christianity has never been a pure brand. In fact, since its inception there has been disagreement on how to share the story of a Jewish
spin-off religion. Schreiter asks, "If contextualization is about getting
to the very heart of the culture, and Christianity is taking its place
there, will not the Christianity that emerges look very much like a
product of that culture?"[30] The earliest example of this problem can be
witnessed in the rift between the apostle Paul and the Jerusalem Jews
led by Peter. As I stated in chapter 5, "Paul's Branding Strategy," the
apostle approached the brand narrative by sharing the gospel through
the cultural context of his audience. On the other hand, Peter and his
colleagues were concerned with the preservation of specific Jewish
tenets—i.e., no unclean meat, circumcision, etc. When we attempt to
share the story of Jesus within the context or framework of another
culture, an altered version of that brand may emerge in order to give
greater meaning to the meta-narrative.

27. Soccio, *Archetypes of Wisdom*, 56–57. Quoted in Viola and Barna, *Pagan
Christianity?*, 89.

28. Ibid.

29. Hatch, *The Influence of Greek*, 113. Quoted in Viola and Barna, *Pagan
Christianity?*, 89.

30. Schreiter, *Constructing Local Theologies*, 150.

EMBRACING THE OTHER

Viola and Barna point out that there is no clear, unadulterated version of Christianity (a.k.a. Christianity Version 1.0). Brian McLaren, a pastor and activist, has written extensively about this subject, "Differentiation is our ability to live separately from others, without being separated . . . The hope is not to defeat, debate, condemn, or even convert the other; rather the hope is to live reconciled with the other, not avoiding differences but seeing them as an expression of the largeness and diverse beauty of God."[31]

The better we understand the "other" (our target audience) we are trying to converse with, the easier the conversation will become. David Kinnaman suggests, "When it comes to interaction with outsiders, we have to realize that our relationships, our interactions with people, comprise the picture of Jesus that people retain."[32] Christianity has worked so diligently to avoid any contamination from the "other" that we have failed to see the commonality that exists—a commonality that could serve as a useful conversation starter.

THE PROBLEM WITH REACHING
THE BIBLICALLY ILLITERATE

There are two issues related to the problem of contextualization. First, ordinary individuals have become more scripturally and spiritually illiterate. Theologian Carlyle Fielding Steward III offers a fine definition of scriptural literacy: "Scriptural literacy does not mean having the ability to readily quote Bible verses to impress others or to show off how religious and righteous we are. Instead it is an intentional, sustained, and systematic examination of the Word of God as part of the spiritual formation and life of any congregation so that the Word may take root in us."[33] Second, clergy have become (too) educated in academia compared to their target audience, thus the gap has widened to monumental proportions.

As the authors of *Made to Stick* point out, the more educated and specialized one becomes in his or her professional field, the harder it is

---

31. Pagitt and Jones, editors, *An Emergent Manifesto*, 143.

32. Kinnaman and Lyons, *UnChristian*, 209.

33. Steward, *Reclaiming What Was Lost*, 31.

for that individual to explain concepts in less complex ways.[34] They note that professionals begin to employ "shop talk," using terms that are commonly understood among peers who share the same educational and professional background. If you have ever had a conversation with an information technology specialist in your institution or congregation, you can easily identify with this phenomenon: You make a phone call requesting assistance regarding a networking problem with your printer, for example. The information technology specialist comes into your office to solve the problem. After about twenty minutes, you are about to lose your mind as he or she "explains" in great detail, using coded language that is all foreign to you. And all the while you're thinking: *All I wanted you to do was fix my printer, not give me a lesson in networking 101!* Complex codes must be broken down into an ordinary lay language that is easy to understand.

As clergy become increasingly educated and specialized in our fields, we unintentionally grow further disconnected from the lives and dealings of ordinary people. B.H. Streeter, twentieth century English theologian and biblical scholar, states, "The Primitive Church had no New Testament, no thought-out theology, no stereotyped traditions. The men who took Christianity to the Gentile world had no special training, only a great experience—in which 'all maxims and philosophies were reduced to the simple task of walking in the light since the light had come.'"[35] David Kinnaman, author of *UnChristian*, suggests that part of the problem is that clergy hold wrong assumptions about what people know about the Bible, which means we often talk about Scripture at a level that people do not understand.

When I was the chaplain of a Christian university, the president of the institution gave his yearly address, defining his vision for the school. He said, "My intention is that this university become a Christocentric institution." He then invited several professors to respond to his speech and explain what they imagined a Christocentric university would look like. Each professor came forward to wax eloquently about his or her belief on living in a Christocentric community. The intellectual divide between the students and the professors was obvious as students sat in the audience, lost. What *does* Christocentric mean? Finally, one professor, who coincidently, taught in the communication department, ex-

34. See Heath and Heath, *Make to Stick*, 206.
35. Quoted in Viola and Barna, *Pagan Christianity?*, 199.

plained the concept to the 18- to 20-year-olds: "To be Christocentric simply means to be Christ-centered." Then he sat down. The students applauded enthusiastically. Some students shouted, "Thanks for making it simple!" The goal for all clergy is to simplify their understanding of theological concepts and contextualize them in relevant language.

The gap in education among clergy and their target audience is further reflected in the Bible translation each prefers. In a nationwide study conducted by the Phoenix, Arizona firm Ellison Research, researchers discovered that the number one Bible choice for pastors is the New International Version (NIV). The findings, which were independently funded, revealed that 39 percent of pastors relied on the NIV as their personal preference and also used it in their work. "The NIV is followed by the traditional King James Version (KJV), which is favored by 24 percent of the pastors. In third place is the New Revised Standard Version (NRSV) at 17 percent, followed by the New King James Version (NKJV) at 10 percent, and the New American Standard (NAS) at 9 percent." Only 2 percent of the clergy indicated a preference for a simpler, more easily understood version such as the New Living Translation, The Message, the Living Bible, the Contemporary English Version, the New Century Version, or the Amplified Bible.[36]

It is interesting to note that the NIV is written at a seventh or eighth grade reading level, while the KJV is ranked at a twelfth grade reading level.[37] According to Amazon.com, the world's largest book retailer, less than half of Americans are able to read at an eighth grade reading level.[38] More discouraging still, nearly 50 percent of Americans surveyed cannot read well enough to find a single piece of information in a short publication, nor can they make low-level inferences based on what they read.[39] In other words, even if they can read the words on the page, they cannot comprehend the ideas being conveyed. Even worse news is that reading scores for American adults of almost all education levels have

36. www.ellisonresearch.com. See also www.crosswalk.com.

37. www.christianbook.com.

38. Amazon.com. See http://askville.amazon.com/average-reading-grade-level-United-States-verifiable-statistic-source/.

39. The National Adult Literacy Survey was the largest study of its kind in 1992 by the National Center for Education Statistics. See Kirsch I.S., Jungeblut A., Jenkins L., Kolstad A. "Adult Literacy in America." National Center for Education Statistics, U. S. Department of Education, September, 1993, Washington, D.C. Accessed on October 12, 2009.

deteriorated, notably among the best-educated groups. From 1992 to 2003, the percentage of adults with graduate school experience who were rated proficient in reading dropped by ten points, a 20 percent rate of decline.[40] If pastors, who are highly educated—most with advanced degrees—prefer to use biblical translations that are well above the reading level of their target audience, how will they articulate the brand in a relevant manner?

CONTEXTUALIZATION IN BIBLICAL TRANSLATION

The methodology of biblical translations may be one of the most pronounced examples of contextualization in Christianity. To translate the Bible one must tell the story in a manner that the target audience understands. This requires adaptation from the original, using modern language, metaphor, and cultural innuendoes that are easily understood by the reader. Bible translators must capture the *spirit* of the biblical narrative while sharing its essential truths in the language of the people reading the Word.

In any given Christian bookstore, there are a couple dozen versions of the Bible on display that boast of being the most accurate translation of the original language. While accuracy is important, it may not be exactly what regular Bible readers are seeking. When the *Living Bible Translation* was first published in 1971, its scholarly integrity was questioned among the critics. However, the LBT version became a best seller because of its accessibility and closeness to the modern language of the day.

BIG BIBLE BUSINESS

The business of Bible sales is a multimillion dollar industry. Publishers of the holy text have carefully analyzed the demographics of potential consumers, and have developed and marketed Bibles based on the look and feel of the product, instead of relying on the traditional black leather bound imprint. Moreover, when publishers put out their tailored version, they can copyright it—something they could not do if they merely reprinted the original. One of the hottest demographics in biblical sales is the teenage market. Repackaging the Bible for that market has been very successful. For example, the controversial *Revolve* and *Refuel*, tab-

40. U.S Department of Education, NCES, *National Assessment of Adult Literacy* (2007). See http://www.nea.gov/news/news07/TRNR.html. Accessed on October 12, 2009.

loid-magazine-like Bibles targeted to girls and boys, respectively, have
been popular. *Revolve*, for instance, sold one hundred and fifty thousand
copies in the first six months of publication.[41] This version of the Bible
mimics a glossy magazine format and is filled with sidebar articles and
tips, from dating to gaining stronger faith.

As a result of increasing Bible sales, publishers now carefully consider how to contextualize the Bible's packaging. Mara Einstein explains
how female marketing is developed in conjunction with Bible sales,
"Because women are the primary purchasers of religious titles, Christian
Living titles cater to their needs and interests, particularly in terms of
family, relationships, and prayer. The importance of women to this market is evidenced by publishing house Thomas Nelson's Women of Faith
division, which sponsors annual motivational conferences to further
support this target audience."[42] Since Bibles continue to lead in all categories of religious sales, the translation used, along with the application
of the Bible, is critical to sales.

Similarly, in 2002 Eugene Peterson published the mega-bestseller
The Message. What made *The Message* so popular? It was the down-to-
earth language that seemed so accessible to both novices and seasoned
readers alike. *The Message* is written at a fifth grade reading level, accessible to most children, teen, and adult readers. Peterson explains, "When
Paul of Tarsus wrote a letter, the people who received it understood it
instantly. When the prophet Isaiah preached a sermon, I can't imagine
that people went to the library to figure it out. That was the basic premise
under which I worked. I began with the New Testament in the Greek—a
rough and jagged language, not so grammatically clean. I just typed
out a page the way I thought it would have sounded to the Galatians."[43]
Peterson's language and expression reflected his personal experience as
a scholar, poet, and pastor. His work vividly captured the ordinary person's grasp of language.

It is interesting to note that while the King James Version and the
New International Version are among the hardest to read in terms of
grade level, they still rank as the best-selling translations based on dollar
sales and unit sales. While they are popular Bibles, the question that

41. Einstein, *Brands of Faith*, 42. See also, Boorstin, *For God's sake. Fortune* magazine, 62.

42. Einstein, *Brands of Faith*, 43.

43. Wikipedia.com.

should be raised is whether the buyers of these books have the ability to comprehend the text? Or are they best sellers because they are used and endorsed by the clergy?

Bible Translations—Based on Dollar Sales

1. New International Version—various publishers
2. King James Version—various publishers
3. New King James Version—various publishers
4. New Living Translation—Tyndale
5. English Standard Version—Crossway
6. Holman Christian Standard Bible—B&H Publishing Group
7. New American Standard Bible update—various publishers
8. New International Reader's Version—Zondervan
9. The Message—Eugene Peterson, NavPress
10. Reina Valera 1960 (Spanish)—American Bible Society and licensees

Bible Translations—Based on Unit Sales

1. New International Version—various publishers
2. New King James Version—various publishers
3. King James Version—various publishers
4. New Living Translation—Tyndale
5. English Standard Version—Crossway
6. Holman Christian Standard Bible—B&H Publishing Group
7. Other Translations
8. New International Reader's Version—Zondervan
9. Reina Valera 1960 (Spanish)—American Bible Society and licensees
10. New American Standard Bible update—various publishers

Contextualization seeks to capture the essence of the meta-narrative instead of the exact detail of the story. The importance here is that the individual understands his or her value in the kingdom of God. The literary success of *The Message* may articulate the desire for the Bible to be written in ordinary language—making it much more accessible to the average person.

When contextualization is practiced, a study of the surrounding community is employed. A right-minded missionary would never go to a foreign country without understanding the cultural nuances, language, popular expressions, and evolving trends. In the same manner, churches should carry out an exhaustive survey to better understand the needs of the community. William Easum suggests a demographics study should be a vital part of congregation's plans of understanding the community.

> Demographics and psychographic studies focus the church outward instead of inward. They tell us who is in the community, which generation or lifestyle is growing or declining, who the church should target, how hard or easy it will be to grow the church, how much income the church could have, and how the church compares to the community. Once a clear picture is formed about the community, the congregation is ready to develop ministries that target some part of it.[44]

JESUS CONTEXTUALIZED THROUGH CODE-SWITCHING

Jesus understood the demographics surrounding his community. The first-century Jews were under the rule of the Roman Empire and were heavily influenced by Hellenistic culture. The Jews were surrounded by multinational influences, just as we are in the West. Jesus was well versed not only in Jewish culture, but also in both Roman and Greek culture. As he traveled throughout Judea, he was able to contextualize his message based on his audience.

Jesus had the ability to code-switch. Code-switching is the ability to decode culture, language, and the use of metaphors conversely within another subculture. Many racial or ethnic minorities are good code-switchers—living at ease within the cultural confines of their neighborhoods, and then switching when they go to work or school among the dominant culture.

---

44. Easum, *Sacred Cows*, 150.

THE WORLD'S GREATEST CODE-SWITCHERS

Some of the greatest leaders had the ability to code-switch throughout the history of the world. Most phenomenal leaders are comfortable in multiple environments. Upon closer examination, leaders who are able to code-switch often grew up or were educated within numerous cultures. For example, Moses, the Old Testament prophet, was proficient in both Jewish and Egyptian cultures. Though born a Jew, he spent his formative years in the queen's palace, where he was educated and indoctrinated in Egyptian culture. In the same way, Indian activist Mahatma *Gandhi* was raised in South Africa and educated in England. Like Moses, Gandhi was an outsider among his own people. While his Indian roots tied him to his race, he understood the cultural nuances of the English mindset. Hence, his ability to code-switch between the two rival cultures was paramount to his ability to negotiate between both sides. When he was among the Indian people, he easily adopted their language, Hindu religion, and customs. But when he was socializing with the political leaders of England, his training as an Oxford educated attorney gave him the leadership edge to communicate in their code and stand on equal footing against his opponents.

MODERN FORM OF CONTEXTUALIZATION

The ability to code-switch is a modern form of contextualization. One must be aware of the dominant culture in which one is immersed and have the ability to speak knowledgeably within that circle. When Jesus traveled through Samaria and conversed with the woman at the well, he was able to code-switch, or contextually speak to her on her grounds.[45] Instead of leveraging the misogynistic culture on his behalf, he gave her the freedom to speak on her terms, where she was comfortable. When he spoke to her, he spoke from her point of view, utilizing her religious and historical background as a common thread in their conversation. However, when Jesus encountered Nicodemus, a high-level Pharisee of the Sanhedrin, in the middle of the night, he was able to code-switch to have a deeper theological conversation.[46] In his conversation with Nicodemus, Jesus explained the plan of salvation concisely, using a very different approach from his approach with the woman at the well.

45. See John 4.
46. See John 3.

Jesus' ability to contextualize the good news was not limited to random conversations. When Jesus renamed Simon as Peter, he did so on the mountain sacred to the Romans in the region of Cesarea Philippi. Here Jesus proclaimed, "You are Peter; and upon this rock I will build my church, and the gates of hell shall not prevail against it" (King James Version).[47] While the majority of his ministry concentrated around the remote villages surrounding the Sea of Galilee, on this occasion Jesus and his disciples made a twenty-five mile trek uphill to the region where multiple religious temples were built in honor of Roman and Hellenistic gods. (Even today, along the side of the mountain where Jesus and his disciples stood are etched carvings of the god *Echo*, the mountain nymph, and *Pan's* consort, along with Pan's father *Hermes*, son of the nymph *Maia*.) The abundant water supply made the region fertile and attractive for worship sites. Jesus was fully aware of his use of metaphor as he stood atop the huge rock (*petros*) and announced, "upon this rock I will build my church." Jesus' use of contextualization here is superb, as through it he simultaneously bridged the three dominant cultures (Jew, Greek, and Roman).

One of the best examples of Jesus' use of contextualization is how he explained "the kingdom of God." Jesus' primary role was to point the human race to his Father. His mission was to explain what the kingdom of God is like. We see his contextualization of this concept throughout the four Gospels. In the parable of the mustard seed, Jesus asks the question twice, "How should I explain what my Father's house is like?"

> Then Jesus asked, "What is the kingdom of God like? What shall I compare it to?
>
> It is like a mustard seed, which a man took and planted in his garden. It grew and became a tree, and the birds of the air perched in its branches."
>
> Again he asked, "What shall I compare the kingdom of God to?"[48]

Depending on the setting, Jesus employed different metaphors to explain the gospel. "He made difficult concepts vivid and used the language of common people to help point them toward spiritual depth. Yet it was not just clever oratorical skills or provocative stories that enthralled people. It was his drive to connect people with God's heart,"

47. See Matthew 16:13–19.

48. See Luke 13:18,19; Mark 4:30–32 13:18–21; Matthew 13:31–33.

explains David Kinnaman.[49] One of Jesus' favorite teaching tools was comparing the kingdom of God in ways that were contemporary, fresh, and relevant to the people around him. Depending on his geographic location, and his audience, he described the kingdom as a secret (Mark 4:11); a growing seed (Mark 4:26); belonging to little children (Mark 10:14, 15); the possession of the poor (Luke 6:20); and open to tax collectors and prostitutes (Matthew 21:43). He contextualized the message to better explain his teachings, based on his audience.

LIVING WITH YOUR AUDIENCE

The use of story was at the heart of Jesus' teaching style. He explained difficult and abstract topics through narrative. This technique is the key to branding a product or message. He was able to articulate his mission in many different ways because he lived among his target audience. Can you imagine if Jesus lived in the urban dwellings of Jerusalem, but ministered among the villages of Galilee on the weekends? His ministry would have suffered. To live in Jerusalem and "commute" the sixty-three miles to Galilee would have been incomprehensible. Because Jesus' ministry centered around Galilee, he settled in that region.

To become contextually relevant within the community you are attempting to reach, it is imperative to live there. Many pastors rely solely on demographics to understand their community. Yes, demographics are critical to better understand the people and culture you are trying to reach, however nothing can substitute living among your target audience. Many pastors and church leaders are attempting a commuter ministry. They live in a different community than the actual community they are attempting to reach.

I have made a personal commitment to live, shop, and play within my local community, as a means of supporting the community and the businesses of Howard County, Maryland. The more time I spend in my community, the stronger the relationships I am able to build with business owners, and the local community. Recently, as I was sitting at one my favorite locally owned coffee shops, a couple passed by me and remarked, "Hey, there's that guy again!" I looked up and greeted them. "We see you everywhere. We feel like we know you." They proceeded to tell me about all of the area bakeries, pastry shops, and coffee lounges

---

49. Kinnaman and Lyons, *UnChristian*, 210.

at which they had seen me in the previous months. The truth is, it can get redundant eating and shopping at the same places; however, this is where the conversations begin that can blossom into relationships. It is where the seeds are sown with people who begin to recognize and trust you. It is where the graphs and data begin to make sense, through personal interactions and conversations.

It is interesting to note that we don't have any written work by Jesus. He didn't create an organizational chart for us to follow, nor did he promote a political agenda, although many expected this of him. "Yet the devotion of the first Christians was powered primarily by their close association with him. He lived and walked among them. They were willing to die for Christ because their loyalty had been forged in their interaction with him," asserts David Kinnaman.[50] Ultimately we have the responsibility to live as Jesus lived. Because we have been commissioned to "go" we must employ the best means to tell the story of Jesus in our community—in a way that our audiences can understand and learn—so that they too will go and brand their faith.

---

50. Kinnaman and Lyons, *UnChristian*, 208.

Bibliography

Adamson, Allen P. *Brand Simple: How the Best Brands Keep it Simple and Succeed.* New York: Palgrave MacMillan, 2006.

"Ailing Starbucks Brings Back Its Architect; Schultz Returns as Company Retrenches." *The Washington Post* (January 8, 2008) sec. DO3.

Aldrich, Joseph C. *Gentle Persuasion: Creative Ways to Introduce your Friends to Christ.* Sisters, OR: Multnomah, 1988.

Alm, Richard. "Women Athletes to Win in Ad Games." *Dallas Morning News* (February 24, 2001).

Bandy, Thomas G. *Christian Chaos: Revolutionizing the Congregation.* Nashville: Abingdon, 1999.

———. *Fragile Hope: Your Church in 2020.* Nashville: Abingdon, 2002.

Banks, Robert. *Paul's Idea of Community.* Revised Edition. Peabody, MA: Hendrickson, 1994.

Barclay, William. *Communicating the Gospel.* Akron, Ohio: St. Andrews Press, 1978.

———. *The Letter to the Romans. Revised Edition.* Philadelphia: Westminster, 1975.

Barna, George. *Marketing the Church,* Colorado Springs: NavPress, 1988.

———. *Transforming Children Into Spiritual Champions: Why Children Should Be Your Church's #1 Priority.* Ventura, CA: Regal, 2003.

Barna Group, The. "A New Generation Expresses its Skepticism and Frustration with Christianity" (September 24, 2007). No pages. Online: http://www.barna.org/barna-update/article/16-teensnext-gen/94-a-new-generation-expresses-its-skepticism-and-frustration-with-christianity

———. "Spiritual Progress Hard to Find in 2003." (December 22, 2003). No pages. Online: http://www.barna.org/barna-update/article/5-barna-update/132-spiritual-progress-hard-to-find-in-2003

Bass, Diana Butler. *Christianity for the Rest of Us: How the Neighborhood Church Is Transforming the Faith.* New York: Harper Collins, 2006.

———. *The Practicing Congregation: Imagining a New Old Church.* Herndon, VA: The Alban Institute, 2004.

Beach, Nancy. *An Hour on Sunday: Creating Moments of Transformation and Wonder.* Grand Rapids: Zondervan, 2004.

Beaudoin, Tom. *Virtual Faith: The Irreverent Spiritual Quest of Generation X.* San Francisco: Jossey-Bass, 1998.

Blake, Chris. *Searching for a God to Love: The One You Always Wanted Is Really There.* Nashville: Word, 2000.

Blanchard, Ken, and Phil Hodges. *Lead Like Jesus: Lessons from the Greatest Leadership Role Model of All Time.* Nashville: Thomas Nelson, 2007.

Blount, Brian K., and Leonora Tubbs Tisdale, editors. *Making Room at the Table: An Invitation to Multicultural Worship.* Louisville: Westminster John Knox, 2000.

Boa, Kenneth, and William Kruidenier. *Romans.* Holman New Testament Commentary. Edited by Max Anders. Nashville: Broadman & Holman, 2000.

Boehlert, Eric. "Bittersweet synergy: Madison Avenue gobbles up rock songs in record numbers." *Rolling Stone* (March 19, 1998), p. 24f.

Bonner, Stanley F. *Education in Ancient Rome: From the Elder Cato to the Younger Pliny.* Berkeley: University of California Press, 1977.

Boorstin, Julia. "For God's Sake Teens open their wallets for a new breed of pop-culture Bible." *Fortune* (November 24, 2003), p. 29.

Bradford, Graeme. "Warning from Ancient Israel." *Adventist Today* (September/October, 2007), p. 12, 13.

Brasher, Brenda E. *Give Me That Online Religion.* San Francisco: Jossey-Bass, 2000.

Breen, Bill. "Who Do You Love?" *Fast Company* (May 2007), p. 82f

Briggs, Rex, and Greg Stuart. *What Sticks: Why Most Advertising Fails and How to Guarantee Yours Succeeds.* Chicago: Kaplan, 2006.

Briner, Robert. *Roaring Lambs: A Gentle Plan to Radically Change Your World.* Grand Rapids: Zondervan, 2000.

Brueggemann, Walter. *The Prophetic Imagination.* Minneapolis: Fortress, 2001.

———. "The liturgy of abundance; the myth of scarcity." *Christian Century* (March 24–31, 1999) p. 342–47.

Buck, Pearl S. *The Good Earth.* New York: Pocket Books, 1931.

Chapman, Anne E., and Kenneth C. Petress. "The Mormons Church and Image Advertising: Appeals for Family Unity and Community Responsibility," The University of Maine. Online: www.umpi.maine.edu/~petress/ArticleH03.pdf.

Cho, David. "The Business of Filling Pews: Congregations Employ Marketing Consultants to Step Up Appeal." *The Washington Post* (March 6, 2005) sec. C01.

Cho, Rebecca U. "Is bottled water a moral issue?" *Christian Century* (January 9, 2007) p. 13–14.

Cohen, Lizabeth. *A Consumers' Republic: The Politics of Mass Consumption in Postwar America.* New York: Alfred A. Knopf, 2003.

Cole, C. L. "The Year That Girls Ruled." *Journal of Sports & Social Issues* 24 (2000) 3.

Collins, Jim. *Good to Great and the Social Sectors: A Monograph to Accompany Good to Great.* New York: Harper Collins, 2005.

Collins, Raymond F. *Introduction to the New Testament.* Garden City: Doubleday, 1983.

Cooke, Phil. *The Last TV Evangelist: Why the Next Generation Couldn't Care Less About Religious Media and Why It Matters.* Huntington Beach, CA: Conversant Media, 2009.

Cowen, Tyler. "Ethnic Goes Exurban: Washington's Sprawl, As Told Through Its Migrating Restaurants." *The Washington Post* (September 3, 2006) sec. B.

Cuneo, Alice Z. "Advertisers Target Women, but Market Remains Elusive." *Advertising Age* (November 10, 1997) p. 1, 24, 26.

Daniels, Cora. "Fast Talk: Coffee Maker Brews Fans." *Fast Company* (July/August 2007) p. 25.

DeYoung, Curtiss Paul, et al., editors. *United by Faith: The Multiracial Congregation as an Answer to the Problem of Race.* New York: Oxford University Press, 2003.

Dockery, David S., editor, *The Challenge of Postmodernism: An Evangelical Engagement.* Grand Rapids: Baker, 1995.

Douglas, J. D., and Philip W. Comfort. *Who's Who in Christian History.* Carol Stream, IL: Tyndale House, 1992.

Dunn, James D. G. *Romans 1–8.* Word Biblical Commentary. Edited by David A. Hubbard. Dallas: Word, 1988.

Easum, William M. *Sacred Cows Make Gourmet Burgers: Ministry Anytime, Anywhere, by Anyone*. Nashville: Abingdon, 1995.

Eberstadt, Nicholas. "Why Poverty Doesn't Rate." *The Washington Post* (September 3, 2006) sec. B01.

Eder, Peter F. "Advertising and mass marketing: the threat and the promise." *The Futurist* (May–June 1990) p. 33 (3).

Einstein, Mara. *Brands of Faith: Marketing Religion in a Commercial Age*. New York: Routledge, 2007.

Eisenstein, Elizabeth L. *The Printing Press as an Agent of Change*. Cambridge, UK: Cambridge University Press.

Elizondo, Virgilio. *The Future Is Mestizo: Life Where Cultures Meet*. Revised Edition. Boulder: University Press of Colorado, 2000.

Erickson, Millard J. *Postmodernizing the Faith: Evangelical Responses to the Challenge of Postmodernism*. Grand Rapids: Baker, 1998.

Erhman, Bart D. *Peter, Paul and Mary Magdalene: The Followers of Jesus in History and Legend*. New York: Oxford University Press, 2008.

Fishman, Charles. "Message in a Bottle." *Fast Company* (July/August 2007). No pages. Online: http://www.fastcompany.com/magazine/117/features-message-in-a-bottle.html.

Friedman, Thomas L. *The World Is Flat: A Brief History of the Twenty-first Century. (Updated and Expanded)*. New York: Farrar, Straus and Giroux, 2006.

Froom, LeRoy E. *Movement of Destiny*. Washington, DC: Review and Herald, 1971.

Gaebelein, Frank E., editor. *Daniel and the Minor Prophets*. The Expositor's Bible Commentary. Grand Rapids: Zondervan, 1976.

Gager, John G. *Reinventing Paul*. Oxford: Oxford University Press, 2000.

Galambush, Julie. *The Reluctant Parting: How the New Testament's Jewish Writers Created a Christian Book*. New York: HarperSanFrancisco 2005.

Garfield, Bob. "YouTube vs. Boob Tube." *Wired* (December 2006), p. 222.

Gaventa, Beverly Roberts. "The Cosmic Power of Sin in Paul's Letter to the Romans: Toward a Widescreen Edition." *Interpretation* (July 2004) p. 229–40.

Gibbs, Eddie. *ChurchNext: Quantum Changes in How We Do Ministry*. Downers Grove, IL: InterVarsity, 2000.

Gilbert, Elizabeth. *Eat, Pray, Love*. New York: Penguin, 2006.

Gillespie, Elizabeth M. "Starbucks Replaces CEO with Chairman." *The Huffington Post* (January 8, 2008) http://www.huffingtonpost.com/huff-wires/20080108/starbucks-ceo/.

Gillespie, V. Bailey. *The Experience of Faith*. Birmingham: Religious Education Press, 1998.

Gladwell, Malcolm. *The Tipping Point: How Little Things Can Make a Big Difference*. New York: Little Brown, 2000.

———. *Blink: The Power of Thinking Without Thinking*. New York: Back Bay, 2005.

Godin, Seth. *All Marketers Are Liars: The Power of Telling Authentic Stories in a Low-Trust World*. New York: Portfolio, 2005.

———. *Tribes: We Need You to Lead Us*. New York: Portfolio. Kindle Edition.

Goldstein, Amy and Dan Keating, "D.C. Suburbs Top List of Richest Counties." *The Washington Post* (August 30, 2006) sec. A01.

Goodson, Dale. "Exchanging, Not Mixing: Contextualization vs. Syncretism, Part II." *Adventist Frontiers* (June 2009) p. 16.

Granderson, Daniel. "Community Will Miss New Hope Church," *Burtonsville Gazette* (July 12, 2006) p. A4, A10.

Grant, Michael. *Saint Paul*. London: Phoenix, 1976.

Green, Joel B., et al., editors. *Dictionary of Jesus and the Gospels*. Downers Grove, IL: InterVarsity, 1992.

Grenz, Stanley J. *A Primer on Postmodernism*. Grand Rapids: Eerdmans, 1996.

Groothuis, Douglas. *Truth Decay: Defending Christianity Against the Challenges of Postmodernism*. Downers Grove, IL: InterVarsity, 2000.

Gugliotto, Lee J. *Handbook for Bible Study: A Guide to Understanding, Teaching, and Preaching the Word of God*. Hagerstown: Review and Herald, 1995.

Guthrie, George H. *Hebrews: The NIV Application Commentary: From Biblical Text . . . to Contemporary Life*. Grand Rapids: Zondervan, 1998.

Hampton, James K. "The Challenge of Postmodernism." *Youth Worker Journal* (January/February 1999) p. 18–24.

Harper, Brad and Paul Louis Metzger. "Here We Are to Worship" *Christianity Today* (August 2009) p. 32(4).

Harris, Dan. "Tempers Flare at Debate on the Devil: Does Satan Exist? Sides Square Off During 'Nightline Face-Off.'" ABC News (March 26, 2009). Online: http://abcnews.go.com/Nightline.

Hatch, Edwin., A. M. Fairbairn, editors. *The Influence of Greek Ideas and Usages Upon the Christian Church: The Hibbert LeHatch Lectures*. London: Williams and Norgate, 1898.

Hays, Richard B. *The Moral Vision of the New Testament. Community, Cross, New Creation, A Contemporary Introduction to New Testament Ethics*. New York: HarperSanFrancisco, 1996.

Healey, James R. "It's hip to be square in Toyota's Scion xB." *USA Today* (March 11, 2004). http://www.usatoday.com/money/autos/reviews/healey/2004-03-11-scion-xb_x.htm.

Heath, Chip, and Dan Heath. *Made to Stick: Why Some Ideas Survive and Others Die*. New York: Random House, 2007.

Heifetz, Ronald A., and Marty Linsky. *Leadership on the Line: Staying Alive Through the Dangers of Leading*. Boston: Harvard Business School Publishing, 2002.

Henderson, David. W. *Culture Shift: Communicating God's Truth to Our Changing World*. Grand Rapids: Baker, 1998.

Herrington, Jim, Mike Bonem, and James Harold Furr. *Leading Congregational Change: A Practical Guide for the Transformational Journey*. San Francisco: Jossey-Bass, 2000.

Hipps, Shane. *The Hidden Power of Electronic Culture: How Media Shapes Faith, the Gospel, and Church*. Grand Rapids: Zondervan, 2005.

Hsu, Albert Y. *The Suburban Christian: Finding Spiritual Vitality in the Land of Plenty*. Downers Grove, IL: InterVarsity, 2006.

Hughes, Mark. *Buzzmarketing: Get People to Talk About Your Stuff*. New York: Penguin, 2005.

Jan, Tracy. "Harvard professor Gates arrested at Cambridge home." *Boston Globe*, July 20, 2009.

Jones, Laurie Beth. *Jesus CEO: Using Ancient Wisdom for Visionary Leadership*. New York: Little Brown, 1996.

Juel, H. Donald. "Multicultural Worship: A Pauline Perspective." In *Making Room at the Table: An Invitation to Multicultural Worship*, edited by Brian K. Blount and Leonora Tubbs Tisdale. Louisville: Westminster John Knox, 2001.

Kaiser, Walter C., Jr. and Moisés Silva. *An Introduction to Biblical Hermeneutics: The Search for Meaning*. Grand Rapids: Zondervan, 1994.

Kates, Steven M., and Glenda Shaw-Garlock. "The Ever Entangling Web: A Study of Ideologies and Discourses in Advertising to Women." *Journal of Advertising* (Summer, 1999) p. 33(1).

Keck, Leander E., editor. *Romans.* The New Interpreter's Bible Vol. 10. Nashville: Abingdon, 2002.

Kenneson, Philip D., and James L. Street. *Selling Out the Church: The Dangers of Church Marketing.* Eugene: Cascade Books, 2003.

Kinnaman, David, and Gabe Lyons. *UnChristian: What a New Generation Really Thinks about Christianity . . . and Why It Matters.* Grand Rapids: Baker, 2007.

Kitchens, Jim. *The Postmodern Parish: New Ministry for a New Era.* Herndon, VA: The Alban Institute, 2003.

Knight, George R. *The Abundant Life Bible Amplifier.* Romans. Boise: Pacific, 1996.

———. *I Used to Be Perfect: A Study of Sin and Salvation.* Second Edition. Berrien Springs, MI: Andrews University Press, 2001.

———. *A User-Friendly Guide to the 1888 Message.* Hagerstown, ML: Review and Herald, 1998.

Kouzes, James M., and Barry Z. Posner. *The Leadership Challenge: How to Keep Getting Extraordinary Things Done in Organizations.* San Francisco: Jossey-Bass, 1995.

Kreider, Alan. *Worship and Evangelism in Pre-Christendom.* Cambridge, UK: Grove, 1995.

Lee, Louise. "Nike Tries Getting in Touch with Its Feminine Side." *Business Week* (October 30, 2000) p. 139.

Lewis, J. Jacqueline. "Struggling with Boundaries in the 21st Century." *Congregations* (Summer 2003) p. 10.

Lewis, Robert, and Wayne Cordeiro. *Culture Shift: Transforming Your Church from the Inside Out.* San Fransisco: Jossey-Bass, 2005.

Lindstrom, Martin. *Brand Sense: Build Powerful Brands through Touch, Taste, Smell, Sight, and Sound.* New York: Free Press, 2005.

Lipset, Seymour Martin. "Comment on Luckmann." In *Social Theory for a Changing Society,* edited by Pierre Bourdieu and James S. Coleman. Boulder: Westview, 1991.

MacArthur, John. "A Challenge for Christian Communicators." *The Master's Seminary Journal* (Spring 2006) p. 7–15.

Mack, Burton L. *Who Wrote the New Testament: The Making of the Christian Myth.* New York: HarperSanFrancisco 1995.

MacLean, Mark. "Worship: Pilgrims in the Faith." In *The Emerging Christian Way: Thoughts, Stories, and Wisdom for a Faith of Transformation,* edited by Michael Schwartzentruber. Kelowna, BC: CopperHouse, 2006.

Maidment, Paul. "Lakshmi Mittal's $19 Billion Year." *Forbes* (March 10, 2005). No pages. Online: http://www.forbes.com.

Martoia, Ron. *Morph: The Texture of Leadership for Tomorrow's Church.* Loveland, CO: Group, 2003.

Mattingly, Terry, and Mark Joseph. *Pop Goes Religion: Faith in Popular Culture.* Nashville: Thomas Nelson, 2005.

Maxwell, John C. *Developing the Leader Within You.* Nashville: Thomas Nelson, 1993.

Mazel, Ella, editor. *And Don't Call Me a Racist! A Treasury of Quotes on the Past, Present, and Future of the Color Line in America.* Lexington, KY: Argonaut, 1998.

McConnell, Ben, and Jackie Huba. *Creating Customer Evangelists: How Loyal Customers Become a Volunteer Sales Force.* Revised Edition. Chicago: Kaplan, 2007.

McCormick, Blaine, and David Davenport. *Shepherd Leadership: Wisdom for Leaders from Psalms 23.* San Francisco: Jossey-Bass, 2003.

McLaren, Brian D. "Church Emerging: Or Why I Still Use the Word Postmodern But with Mixed Feelings" in An Emergent Manifesto of Hope eds., Doug Pagitt and Tony Jones (Grand Rapids, Michigan: Baker Books, 2007).

————. *The Church on the Other Side: Exploring the Radical Future of the Local Church.* Revised and expanded edition of *Reinventing Your Church.* Grand Rapids: Zondervan, 2006.

————. *More Ready Than You Realize: Evangelism As Dance In the Postmodern Matrix.* Grand Rapids: Zondervan, 2002.

McLuhan, Marshall. *The Gutenberg Galaxy: The Making of Typographic Man.* Toronto: University of Toronto Press, 1962.

McManus, Erwin Raphael. *The Barbarian Way: Unleash the Untamed Faith Within.* Nashville: Thomas Nelson, 2005.

Meacham, Jon. "The End of Christian America." *Newsweek* (April 13, 2009) p. 34.

Meeks, Wayne A. *The First Urban Christians: The Social World of the Apostle Paul.* New Haven: Yale University Press, 1983.

"Methodists Plan Another Ad Campaign." *Christian Century* (March 8, 2005) p. 17.

Metzger, Bruce M. *The New Testament: Its Background, Growth, and Content.* Second Edition. Nashville: Abingdon, 1983.

Michel, Ann A. "Young Adults and the Future of the Church." *Leading Ideas Newsletter,* Lewis Center for Church Leadership, Wesley Theological Seminary, 2007.

Michelli, Joseph A. *The Starbucks Experience: 5 Principles for Turning Ordinary into Extraordinary.* New York: McGraw-Hill, 2007.

Miller, Donald. *Blue Like Jazz: Nonreligious Thoughts on Christian Spirituality.* Nashville: Thomas Nelson, 2003.

Mullen, Lisa Takeuchi. "Stretching for Jesus." *Time* (August 29, 2005). http://www.time .com/time/magazine/article/0,9171,1098937,00.html.

Murrow, David. *Why Men Hate Going to Church.* Nashville: Thomas Nelson, 2005.

Nam, Julius. "Adventism in Present Communal Progressive." *Adventist Today* (September/ October, 2007) p. 8–10.

Navarro, Xavier. "Detroit church turns Sunday into SUV-day with prayer for auto industry." (Dec 9, 2008). No pages. Online: http://green.autoblog.com/2008/12/09 /detroit-church-uses-hybrids-to-pray-for-the-health-of-the-auto-i/.

Newman, J. David. "Adventist Church Found Wanting." *Adventist Today* (September/ October, 2007) p. 14–17.

Ngeo, Christine. "The First Gatekeeper: Healthcare Ads Target Women as Key Decisionmakers." *Modern Healthcare* 28 (July 6, 1998) p. 34 (1).

Norrington, David C. *To Preach or Not.* London: Paternoster, 1997.

Oden, Amy G. *God's Welcome: Hospitality for a Gospel-Hungry World.* Pilgrim, 2008.

O'Rourke, P. J. "Venti Capitalists." *The New York Times* (December 16, 2007) p. 10L.

Pagitt, Doug, and Tony Jones, editors. *An Emergent Manifesto of Hope.* Grand Rapids: Baker, 2008.

Paulien, Jon. "God's Mighty Acts in a Changing World." *Ministry* (February, 2006) p. 10–12.

Paulsen, Jan. "The Openness That Lies Before Us." *Adventist World-NAD* (October, 2006) p. 8–10.

Penner, Myron Bradley, and Hunter Barnes, editors. *A New Kind of Conversation.* London: Paternoster, 2007.

Power, Carla. "Lost in Silent Prayer." *Newsweek* [European edition] (July 12, 1999) p. 48.

Prehn, Yvon. *Ministry Marketing Made Easy: A Practical Guide to Marketing Your Church Message.* Nashville: Abingdon, 2004.

Puskas, Charles B. *An Introduction to the New Testament.* Peabody, MA: Hendrickson, 1999.

Putnam, Robert D. *Bowling Alone: The Collapse and Revival of American Community.* New York: Simon & Schuster, 2000.

Quinn, Robert E. *Deep Change: Discovering the Leader Within.* San Francisco: Jossey-Bass, 1996.

Rabey, Steve. *In Search of Authentic Faith: How Emerging Generations are Transforming the Church.* Colorado Springs: Waterbrook, 2001.

Rainer, Thom S. *The Unchurched Next Door.* Grand Rapids: Zondervan, 2003.

————. *Surprising Insights from the Unchurched and Proven Ways to Reach Them.* Grand Rapids: Zondervan, 2001.

Reising, Richard L. *Church Marketing 101: Preparing Your Church for Greater Growth.* Grand Rapids: Baker, 2006.

"Religious Americans: My Faith isn't the only way: Survey shows growing religious tolerance when it comes to different faiths." The Associated Press (June 23, 2008). No pages. Online: MSNBC.com.

Rice, Richard. *Believing, Behaving, Belonging: Finding New Love for the Church.* Roseville: The Association of Adventist Forums, 2002.

Richardson, Rick. *Evangelism Outside the Box: New Ways to Help People Experience the Good News.* Downers Grove, IL: InterVarsity, 2000.

Richtel, Matt. "At Starbucks, Songs of Instant Gratification." *The New York Times* (October 1, 2007) p. C1.

Ries, Al, and Laura Ries. *The Origin of Brands: Discover the Natural Laws of Product Innovation and Business Survival.* New York: HarperBusiness, 2004.

Ritter, Karl. "World's Oldest Newspaper Goes Digital." (February 5, 2007). No pages. Online: http://news.yahoo.com/s/ap/20070205/ap_on_hi_te/sweden_oldest_newspaper.

Rivkin, Steve, and Fraser Sutherland. *The Making of a Name: The Inside Story of the Brands We Buy.* Oxford: Oxford University Press, 2004.

Romanowski, William D. *Pop Culture Wars: Religion & the Role of Entertainment in American Life.* Downers Grove, IL: InterVarsity, 1996.

Roxburgh, Alan J., and Fred Romanuk. *The Missional Leader: Equipping Your Church to Reach a Changing World.* San Francisco: Jossey-Bass, 2006.

Sahlin, Monte. *Adventist Congregations Today: New Evidence for Equipping Healthy Churches.* Lincoln, NE: Center for Creativity Ministry, 2003.

————. "The Adventist Church in North America Today." *Adventist Today* (September/October 2007) p. 6–8.

————. *Understanding Your Community: Intuitive Assessment Tools to Launch Relevant Ministry.* Lincoln, NE: Center for Creative Ministry, 2004.

Salzman, Nathaniel. "The New Stewards: Rebranding Adventism," *Mid-America Outlook* (July 2007) p. 6.

Sanders, E. P. *Paul: A Very Short Introduction.* Oxford: Oxford University Press, 1991.

————. *Paul and Palestinian Judaism: A Comparison of Patterns of Religion.* Minneapolis: Fortress, 1977.

Schaller, Lyle E. *Create Your Own Future!: Alternatives for the Long-Range Planning Committee.* Nashville: Abingdon, 1991.

————. *The Very Large Church.* Nashville: Abingdon, 2000.

Schley, Bill, and Carl Nichols Jr. *Why Johnny Can't Brand: Rediscovering the Lost Art of the Big Idea.* New York: Portfolio, 2005.

Schreiner, Thomas R. *Paul: Apostle of God's Glory in Christ.* Downers Grove, IL: InterVarsity, 2001.

Schreiter, Robert J. *Constructing Local Theologies.* Maryknoll: Orbis, 1985.

Schulte, Brigid. "Shrinking Flock Examines Its Identity: Churches Renamed to Escape Stigma Some Say 'Baptist' Carries." *The Washington Post* (June 8, 2008) sec. C01.

Schwarz, Christian A. *Natural Church Development: A Guide to Eight Essential Qualities of Healthy Churches.* Carol Stream, IL: ChurchSmart Resources, 1996.

Schwartz, J. "Stalking the Youth Market." *Newsweek* (Summer/Fall 1990) p. 34 (3).

Schwartzentruber, Michael, editor. *The Emerging Christian Way: Thoughts, Stories and Wisdom for a Faith of Transformation.* Kelowna, BC: CopperHouse, 2006.

Segal, Alan F. *Paul the Convert: The Apostolate and Apostasy of Saul the Pharisee.* New Haven: Yale University Press, 1990.

Senge, Peter M. *The Fifth Discipline: The Art and Practice of the Learning Organization.* New York: Currency Doubleday, 2006.

Seybold, Patricia B., *Customers.com: How to Create a Profitable Business Strategy for the Internet and Beyond.* New York: Random House, 1998.

"Shares tumble 5% after downgrade." *Chicago Tribune* (December 18, 2007) p. B2.

Shawchuck, Norman, and Philip Kotler, et al. *Marketing for Congregations: Choosing to Serve People More Effectively.* Nashville: Abingdon, 1992.

Shenk, David W. and Linford Stutzman, eds. *Practicing Truth: Confident Witness in Our Pluralistic World.* Scottsdale, PA: Herald Press, 1999.

Sider, Ronald J. *The Scandal Of The Evangelical Conscience: Why Are Christians Living Just Like The Rest Of The World?* Grand Rapids: Baker, 2005.

———. *Rich Christians in an Age of Hunger: Moving from Affluence to Generosity.* Dallas: Word, 1997.

Slaughter, Michael, with Warren Bird. *Unlearning Church.* Loveland, CO: Group, 2001.

Soccio, Douglas J. *Archetypes of Wisdom: An Introduction to Philosophy.* Belmont, CA: Wadsworth/ITP, 1998.

Stadler, Kathleen M., and Jumanah S. Essa. "The ABC's of Eating Out." Virginia Cooperative Extension (June 2001). No Pages. Online: http://www.ext.vt.edu /pubs/nutrition/348-951/34-51.html.

Stafford, Tim. "Making Do with More." *Christianity Today* (February 2006), p. 58(4).

Stamler, Bernard. "Sex Appeal still Overpowers Sports Skill when It Comes to the Marketing of Female Athletes." *The New York Times* (August 9, 2000) sec. C2.

Stanley, Andy. *Visioneering: God's Blueprint for Developing and Maintaining Personal Vision.* Sisters: Multnomah, 1999.

Stevens, Tim, and Tony Morgan. *Simply Strategic Growth: Attracting a Crowd to Your Church.* Loveland, CO: Group, 2005.

Stevens, Tim. *Pop Goes the Church: Should the Church Engage in Pop Culture?* Indianapolis: Power, 2008.

Stewart, Carlyle Fielding, III. *Reclaiming What Was Lost: Recovering Spiritual Vitality in the Mainline Church.* Nashville: Abingdon, 2003.

Stone, Howard, and James O. Duke. *How to Think Theologically.* Minneapolis: Fortress, 1996.

Stott, John. *Romans: God's Good News for the World.* Downers Grove, IL: InterVarsity, 1994.

Strobel, Lee. *Inside The Mind of Unchurched Harry and Mary: How to Reach Friends and Family Who Avoid God and the Church.* Grand Rapids: Zondervan, 1993.

Stuessy, Joe, and Scott D. Lipscomb. *Rock And Roll: Its History and Stylistic Development.* Third Edition. Upper Saddle River, NJ: Prentice Hall, 1999.

Sugirtharajah, R. S., editor. *Voices from the Margin: Interpreting the Bible in the Third World.* New Edition. Maryknoll: Orbis, 1995.

Surowiecki, James. *The Wisdom of Crowds.* New York: Anchor, 2005.

Sweet, Leonard. *Summoned to Lead*. Grand Rapids: Zondervan, 2004.

———. *Soul Tsunami: Sink or Swim in the New Millennium Culture*. Grand Rapids: Zondervan, 1999.

Sweet, Leonard, Brian D. McLaren, and Jerry Haselmayer. *A Is for Abductive: The Language of the Emerging Church*. Grand Rapids: Zondervan, 2003.

Swindoll, Charles R. *Paul: A Man of Grace and Grit*. Nashville: Thomas Nelson, 2002.

Thomson, Jeremy. *Preaching as Dialogue: Is the Sermon a Sacred Cow?* Cambridge: Grove Books, 1996.

Trenchard, Warren C. *Complete Vocabulary Guide to the Greek New Testament*. Revised Edition. Grand Rapids: Zondervan, 1998.

Turow, Joseph. *Niche Envy: Marketing Discrimination in the Digital Age*. London: The MIT Press, 2006.

Twitchell, James B. *Branded Nation: The Marketing of Megachurch, College Inc., and Museumworld*. New York: Simon & Schuster, 2004.

Viola, Frank, and George Barna. *Pagan Christianity? Exploring the Roots of Our Church Practices*. Carol Stream, IL: Tyndale House, 2008.

Vitello, Paul. "Bad Times Draw Bigger Crowds to Churches." *New York Times* (December 14, 2008) p.

Waltz, Mark L. *First Impressions: Creating Wow Experiences in Your Church*. Loveland, CO: Group, 2005.

Warren, Rick. "Evangelizing the 21st Century Culture." Pastors.com. No pages. Online: www.pastors.com.

Weber, Martin. *Adventist Hot Potatoes*. Boise: Pacific, 1991.

Weems, Lovett H., Jr. *Church Leadership: Vision, Team, Culture and Integrity*. Nashville: Abingdon, 1993.

Wenham, David. *Paul: Follower of Jesus or Founder of Christianity?* Grand Rapids: Eerdmans, 1995.

Wheatley, Margaret J. *Leadership and the New Science: Discovering Order in a Chaotic World*. San Francisco: Berrett-Koehler, 2006.

White, Ellen G. *Testimonies for the Church*. Volume 9. Mountain View, ID: Pacific, 1942.

———. *Testimonies to Ministers and Gospel Workers*. Mountain View, ID: Pacific, 1923.

———. *Christ's Object Lessons*. Washington DC: Review and Herald, 1900.

Wiklander, Bertil. "Understanding Secular Minds: A Perspective on 'Life Development.'" *Ministry* (March 2003) p. 12–15.

Wills, Garry. *What Paul Meant*. New York: Viking, 2006.

Winston, William, Robert E. Stevens, and David L. Loudon, *Marketing for Churches and Ministries*. Florence, KY: Routledge, 1996.

Witherington, Ben, III. *The Paul Quest: The Renewed Search for the Jew of Tarsus*. Downers Grove, IL: InterVarsity, 1998.

Woolever, Cynthia, and Deborah Bruce. *Beyond the Ordinary: Ten Strengths of U.S. Congregations*. Louisville: Westminster John Knox, 2004.

Wuthnow, Robert. *After the Baby Boomers*. Princeton, NJ: Princeton University Press, 2007.

Zezima, Katie. "A New Emphasis for the Ministry: Management Skills." *The New York Times* (December 15, 2007) p. B5(L).

Zoll, Rachel. "More Americans say they have no religion." The Associated Press (March 9, 2009). No pages. Online: http://www.newsvine.com/_news/2009/03/08/2521636-more-americans-say-they-have-no-religion

Scripture Index

Subject/Name Index

About the Author

Rajkumar Dixit is a nationally recognized speaker and trainer, specializing in branding and leadership development. He serves as an associate pastor at New Hope Adventist Church where he oversees the administration, missions, and community development of the church. He earned his Doctor of Ministry at Wesley Theological Seminary, in Washington, DC, with an emphasis in leadership, focusing on religious and nonprofit branding. Dr. Dixit also teaches courses in religion and communication at Washington Adventist University. He is married to Rajinie, and the father of Jaelin, Elijah, and Wilomina. He resides in Howard County, Maryland.

All author proceeds from this book will be donated to Sharing Our Strength (S.o.S.), the missions ministry of New Hope Church. S.o.S. focuses on international outreach to Mozambique and Haiti and local outreach initiatives within the communities surrounding New Hope Church. To learn more, visit www.newhopesos.blogspot.com.

To download a free discussion guide to this book, visit rajkumar dixit.com.